Microsoft Flight Simulator 2024 Handbook

A Comprehensive Guide to Customization, World Exploration, Advanced Techniques and Realistic Flight for the Optimal Flight Experience

Ben Calvin

OVERVIEW

On November 19, 2024, Microsoft flight Simulator 2024, the newest version of flight simulation, was made available. For the first time, a full career mode from publisher Xbox Game Studios and developer Asobo Studio lets players take on a variety of aviation-related tasks, including crop dusting, search and rescue operations, and aerial firefighting. Utilizing cutting-edge simulation, cloud computing, machine learning, graphics, and gaming technologies, the game offers a unique experience. One of the many fantastic characteristics of Microsoft Flight Simulator 2024 is its improved, realistic, and more advanced game engine. In order to display terrains with genuine geographical and other environmental aspects in mind, it supports a new online machine-learning platform that generates terrain detail in real-time according to a set of predetermined criteria supplied by the developer. This makes the terrains realistic and authentic. In addition to the technical advancement, the simulator will have a large range of aircraft, including gliders, hot air balloons, antique combat planes, and commercial airliners. Users will be able to experience all aspects of aviation, ranging from professional simulation to flying at a hobbyist level. Aerial firefighting and search and rescue are two more mission kinds that enhance the gameplay for difficult and captivating user situations. Additionally, with the help of cloud streaming technologies, Microsoft Flight Simulator 2024's installation size was reduced to around 30GB. Because users can now stream all the high-quality data without the need for substantial local storage, it makes the flight simulator more accessible to a wider audience. Before we begin, it is crucial to understand that Microsoft Flight Simulator will be referred to as MSFS 2024 throughout this article.

CHAPTER ONE

OVERVIEW OF THE 2024 MICROSOFT FLIGHT SIMULATOR

An Overview of Flight Simulation

Building on the solid basis established by its predecessor in 2020, the introduction of Microsoft Flight Simulator 2024 has signaled and established a significant milestone in the world of flight simulation. The additional features and enhancements in this edition, which was created by Asobo Studio and released by Xbox Game Studios, are intended to benefit both seasoned pilots and those who are new to flight simulation.

Better Career Mode

Microsoft Flight Simulator 2024's extensive, detailed career mode is its most intriguing feature. Aerial firefighting, search and rescue, helicopter freight transport, air ambulance services, crop dusting, mountain rescue, skydiving, and commercial aviation are just a few of the aviation occupations that fall under this umbrella. Each adds even more complexity and realism to the game, but they also present various obstacles and need separate in-game certificates.

A Wide Range of Aircraft

Over 70 superbly made, highly detailed aircraft - from gliders and hot air balloons to commercial giants like the Boeing 747-400 LCF Dreamlifter - are featured in its basic version, out of the box. Every one of them will keep one interested in all facets of flying, from simple sightseeing to the finer points of a commercial trip.

Suppressing Visual Enhancements

In terms of visual realism, Microsoft Flight Simulator 2024 keeps getting better. This simulator maps the whole world in incredible detail using advanced procedural generation methods and high-resolution satellite photos straight from Bing Maps. A new photometric lighting system adds to its realism by capturing the right weather and time of day. Players are further immersed in the virtual sky by dynamic meteorological events, such as wildfires, tornadoes, and auroras.

Enhanced Accessibility and Performance

This edition's significant installation size decrease is one of its most notable features. The simulator's installation size has decreased from the 150GB needed by its predecessor to around 30GB due to advancements in cloud streaming technologies. For many users, this lowers the entrance barrier and greatly facilitates installation.

Realistic Flight Dynamics and Systems

The development team has been working hard to improve aircraft systems and flying dynamics. The electrical, pneumatic, fuel, and hydraulic systems have been redesigned for a considerably more realistic flying experience, and the new physics engine makes way for much greater control with add-on-created flight dynamics. These improvements guarantee that every aircraft operates in unison with its real-world counterpart and provide pilots of all skill levels a demanding but rewarding experience.

Support from the Community and Third Parties

The support for community-generated material in Microsoft Flight Simulator 2024 is similarly robust. To ensure that the sizable developer and modder community can continue to expand and grow the simulator with more content and experiences for its players, Microsoft has stated that "virtually all" add-ons purchased through the Flight Simulator online marketplace for the previous version will function in the new release.

Reaction and Prospects for the Future

When Microsoft Flight Simulator 2024 was released, it was mostly well-reviewed, with many praising its realistic flight dynamics, multiple career paths, and enhanced graphics. On launch day, however, things weren't quite easy. The servers were overcrowded with gamers, which resulted in lengthy loading times and virtual lines. The development team quickly resolved these, and in order to ensure that every user has a seamless experience, they have subsequently expanded server capacity and are focusing on speed optimization. Microsoft aviation Simulator 2024 will continue to be a staple in the aviation simulation industry. With its appealing mix of accessibility and realism, as well as the ecosystem of third-party material that supports it, the title stands for the unparalleled platform that virtual aviators use to take off. From the first click to the last, Microsoft Flight Simulator 2024 is a comprehensive and immersive aviation experience that sets the standard high for its class, catering to both experienced pilots and novices just learning the ropes.

System Installation and Requirements

One of the biggest advancements in aviation simulation is Microsoft aviation Simulator 2024. This version has a lot of new features in addition to previously unheard-of realism. Understanding the system requirements and installation procedures is necessary to be ready for such a wonderful experience.

System prerequisites

A number of hardware setups that fit within the Minimum, Recommended, and Ideal Spec categories can operate the MSFS 2024.

Microsoft Flight Simulator 2024	MIN SPEC		RECOMMENDED SPEC		IDEAL SPEC	
	AMD	NVIDIA/INTEL	AMD	NVIDIA/INTEL	AMD	NVIDIA/INTEL
MIN OS VERSION	Windows 10 With latest update	Windows 10 With latest update	Windows 10 With latest update	Windows 10 With latest update	Windows 10 With latest update	Windows 10 With latest update
DIRECT X VERSION	DX12	DX12	DX12	DX12	DX12	DX12
CPU	AMD Ryzen 5 2600X	Intel Core i7-6800K	AMD Ryzen 7 2700X	Intel Core i7-10700K	AMD Ryzen 7 7900X	Intel i7-14700K
GPU	Radeon RX 5700	GeForce GTX 970	Radeon RX 5700 XT	GeForce RTX 2080	Radeon RX 7900 XT	GeForce RTX 4080
VRAM	4 GB	4 GB	8 GB	8 GB	12 GB	12 GB
RAM	16 GB	16 GB	32 GB	32 GB	64 GB	64 GB
STORAGE	50 GB	50 GB	50 GB	50 GB	50 GB	50 GB
BANDWIDTH	10 Mbps	10 Mbps	50 Mbps	50 Mbps	100 Mbps	100 Mbps

Minimum Requirements

- **Operating System:** Windows 10 with the latest updates
- **DirectX:** Version 12
- **CPU:** AMD Ryzen 5 2600X or Intel Core i7-6800K
- **GPU:** AMD Radeon RX 5700 or NVIDIA GeForce GTX 970
- **VRAM:** 4 GB
- **RAM:** 16 GB
- **Storage:** 50 GB
- **Internet Bandwidth:** 10 Mbps

By using these minimal requirements, the simulator's settings will be lowered, resulting in a more basic user experience that will work well with outdated technology.

Suggested Specifications

- **Operating System:** Windows 10
- **DirectX:** Version 12
- **CPU:** AMD Ryzen 7 2700X or Intel Core i7-10700K
- **GPU:** AMD Radeon RX 5700 XT or NVIDIA GeForce RTX 2080
- **VRAM:** 8 GB
- **RAM:** 32 GB
- **Storage:** 50 GB
- **Internet Bandwidth:** 50 Mbps

You may use the simulator at higher settings if your system meets these suggested specs, which will result in smoother performance and greater visual quality. It should be mentioned that a Solid State Drive (SSD) is strongly recommended even if the storage requirement calls for 50 GB for each of them. Your simulation experience will be improved by an SSD, which will significantly speed up loading times and increase overall performance.

How to Set Up

Whether you buy a hard or digital copy of Microsoft Flight Simulator 2024, installing it is rather easy.

- **Buy and download:**
  - **Digital Edition:** This may be found on a number of websites, including Steam and the Microsoft Store. The installer is available for download from the selected platform after purchase.

- ➢ **Physical Edition:** If you have a physical copy, start the installation procedure by putting the installation disk into the computer's drive.
- ♦ **Procedures for Installation:**
  - ➢ **Launch Installer:** Launch the installer and adhere to the prompts on the screen.
  - ➢ **Choose Installation Path:** Decide on the installation directory of your choice. Selecting a disk with at least 50 GB of free space is essential, but even more is advised if you want to download more updates and content.
  - ➢ **Download More Content:** For high-detail sections and real-time data, MSFS 2024 uses cloud streaming technology. The simulator could download some necessary files while it is being installed. During this stage, a reliable internet connection is essential.
- ♦ **Patches and Updates:** Additional updates and patches will be downloaded after the installation is finished. The majority of these changes are made to guarantee that every feature is used to its maximum capacity. Before opening, wait for the download and installation to finish.
- ♦ **Configuration:**
  - ➢ **Graphic Settings:** MSFS 2024 automatically identifies hardware and recommends settings based on its best judgment when you launch it for the first time. These may always be changed to balance visual quality with performance.
  - ➢ **Control Setup:** To guarantee smooth flight, the first step in playing this game is to configure your favorite input devices, such as a gamepad, joystick, or yoke.

Enhancing Efficiency

The following advice will assist in achieving optimal success in MSFS 2024:
- ♦ **Update Drivers:** It is necessary to update the drivers for the graphics card and other important pieces of hardware. Companies often provide upgrades to make their software more compatible and seamless with the most recent versions.
- ♦ **Modify Graphics Settings:** If you have performance problems, think about reducing anti-aliasing, shadow detail, and texture quality. This change may result in more fluid gameplay without appreciably sacrificing visual quality.
- ♦ **Track System Resources:** Keep an eye on CPU, GPU, and RAM use by using task management tools. System resources may be freed up by shutting off unused background apps, improving simulator performance.
- ♦ **Internet Connection:** Since MSFS 2024 feeds real-time weather, traffic, and terrain data, a dependable and quick internet connection is essential. Using a

wired connection or upgrading your internet subscription might provide a more dependable experience.

Using the User Interface

The updated user interface (UI) of Microsoft Flight Simulator 2024 (MSFS 2024) is intended to improve user experience and simplify navigation.

Overview of the Main Menu

The globe is highlighted in the very visually appealing main menu when the user first launches MSFS 2024. While showcasing new modes, it still makes accessing free flights and traditional activities fast and simple. In addition to displaying the username, the profile area in the upper right offers access to the in-sim Marketplace, settings, alerts, and a messaging service. The pilot profile, which displays career development, challenge league ranks, and other pertinent data, is shown when the username is clicked.

Free Flight and Activities

Among other things, the Activities menu's horizontal scroll interface leads players through low-altitude challenges, rally races, and flying instruction. Although it is more organized, the Free Flight portion still has the same layout. There is more visibility and accessibility to the selection and configuration of aircraft as well as the modification of flying conditions.

Aircraft Configuration and Selection

Users may browse, search, sort, and filter aircraft on the selection page, including Marketplace purchases. Selecting liveries, switching out variations, and obtaining aircraft data are all part of the 'Configure' option. In addition, payload may be changed in this menu and other settings with visual elements, including installing engine covers and chocks on the aircraft, which can be done in free flight using the walk-around mode.

World Map and Flight Conditions

It allows for live, preset, or custom flying circumstances, including weather and time. Most significantly, it included a feature that would allow users to customize the weather and air traffic over the last 24 hours in MSFS 2024, which will make flying more realistic and dynamic. Major airports and other areas of interest are prominently indicated for convenient navigation and flight planning, and the World Map's design remains user-friendly.

Universal Electronic Flight Bag (EFB) with In-Flight Toolbar

After being undocked, the toolbar is redesigned to match the main menu's aesthetic. The most significant addition is the global EFB by Working Title, which significantly enhances in-flight management and situational awareness by including flight information, procedures, cargo statistics, and much more for every aircraft.

Interface for Controller Settings

A recently updated controller settings interface is a part of MSFS 2024. Categories like "General controls," "Airplane controls," and "Specific airplane name controls" are among its pillars. A wide range of customized control profiles are made possible by this hierarchy to support common aircraft controls, general instructions, and special features unique to each aircraft type. As users have noted, successfully setting peripherals in pursuit of individual flying experiences requires a comprehension of this hierarchy.

Community Input and Adjustment

The community's response to the new user interface has been conflicting. While some find it less straightforward in certain ways, including as attempting to modify controller settings, others like the sleeker, more sophisticated appearance. Discussion threads highlight the need to import control schemes from previous versions and challenges with peripheral configuration. For further information and solutions to common problems, community forum discussions and official FAQs might be helpful.

Comprehending the Main Menu

The secret to a fantastic flight simulation experience comprehends the design and operation of this menu.

Overview of the Main Menu

The primary menu, which is slick and easy to use, is shown on a splash screen that fades in as MSFS 2024 loads. **It is broken up into several important portions that lead to different parts of the simulator:**

- **Home:** This page offers quick access to news updates, highlighted activities, and recent flights. With easy access to well-known locations and challenges, it's the default tab for the majority of users.
- **World Map:** Pilots may arrange flights on this tab by selecting a point of departure and arrival, assessing flying conditions, and altering routes as necessary. To make flight planning more realistic, the interactive map also shows current weather and air traffic.
- **Activities:** This section offers a wide range of tasks, lessons, and challenges to test one's flying abilities. The list is limitless and includes anything from landing difficulties to wilderness treks.
- **Profile:** A user's flying history, accomplishments, and pilot profile are all accessible here. Here, you may also adjust preferences and settings to personalize the simulation experience.

9

- **Options:** All of the controls, sound, graphics, and general preferences are stored here. By adjusting them, you may improve performance and add some personalization to the simulator.
- **Marketplace:** To improve their simulation experience, customers may purchase extra material including aircraft, liveries, and landscape modifications from this integrated shop.

Using the Main Menu

Because each component has tabs or icons that are clearly identified, navigating the main menu is rather simple. The main parts may be quickly accessed from the top navigation bar, and each area has submenus that let users go further into specifics.

- **Home Button:** Shown by a home symbol in the upper left corner, this button facilitates fast navigation back to the beginning point by taking users from any subpage to the main menu.
- The buttons for back and close are in the lower-left corner. For quicker access to settings and choices, the buttons enable users to 'exit' or return to any previous menu.

Changing the Settings

Here, the following options are essential for customizing the simulator to the user's preferences:
- **General Options:** Modify the traffic, data use, accessibility, and graphical settings. If these parameters are further adjusted, improved performance and higher visual quality should result.

10

- **Help Options:** Depending on your skill level, turn on or off the in-sim aids, such as checklist help, auto-rudder, and others.
- **Controls:** Keyboards, mouse, joysticks, and yokes are among the devices used. To ensure that their control configuration is exactly as they want it, users may assign certain functions to their favorite buttons and axes.

Utilizing the World Map to Plan Flights

The World Map is one of the most reliable resources for flight planning:
- **Choosing Airports:** To choose an airport as a departure or arrival point, click on it. Along with other details, it provides information on runway lengths and ILS availability.
- **Flight Conditions:** To replicate various flight situations, choose the weather, time of day, and other environmental elements.
- **Route Customization:** For flexibility in both VFR and IFR flights, create unique flight plans by choosing preferred airways, adding waypoints, and modifying the cruising altitude.

Getting to Activities

The Activities area contains a variety of material, such as:
- **Flight Training:** Courses intended to impart the fundamentals of aviation navigation, flying, and aircraft control. Excellent for anyone who have never used the simulator before or who want to brush up on their abilities.
- **Bush Trips:** Pilots must navigate prearranged picturesque flights without GPS. Excellent navigational abilities and breathtaking vistas.
- **Landing Challenges:** Put your ability to land various aircraft in various weather circumstances to the test, aiming for accuracy and smoothness.

Controlling Your Profile

In the section on profiles:
- **Logbook:** Comprehensive records of previous flights include the aircraft flown, the time of departure and arrival airports, and the flight duration in order to monitor experience and development.
- **Pilot Profile:** View accomplishments, total flight time, and more data pertaining to your virtual aviation profession.
- **Customization:** For more realism, add your call sign, avatar, and other private details.

Examining the Market

One area of MSFS 2024 where you may broaden your experience is the Marketplace:
- **Add-ons:** Look through and purchase more scenery packs, aircraft, and liveries made by Microsoft and other developers.
- **Content Manager:** To keep your simulator up to date and customized, manage installed add-ons, including updating and removing content.

Resolving Access Problems

Try the following if you are experiencing issues accessing the main menu, such as the screen loading to 100% and stopping there:
- **The Community Folder should be empty**: Third-party add-ons might lead to conflicts. To temporarily delete the Community folder and see if the problem goes away, transfer all of its contents out.
- **Clear Cache:** Occasionally, removing the cache resolves loading problems. Open the Options menu, choose Data, and then search for cache management options to erase the cache. The rolling cache may usually be cleared out or rebuilt to fix problems.
- **Update Simulator:** Make sure Microsoft Flight Simulator 2024 is up to current on your computer. Numerous updates fix issues or stabilize the program as a whole. You may use the launcher for your platform, such as Steam or the Microsoft Store, to check for updates.
- **Verify System Requirements:** Verify that your hardware meets or surpasses the system requirements. Low system performance may be one of the several reasons for graphical defects and poor menu loading.
- **Community Support:** If an issue persists, official Microsoft Flight Simulator forums and community centers such as AVSIM or FlightSim.com are excellent resources for troubleshooting hints and guidance.

Advice for Novice Users

The main menu's abundance of features may be too much for a novice user of Microsoft Flight Simulator 2024 to handle. **The following advice will help you get the most out of your experience:**
- Take the Tutorials: Start by taking the flying instruction courses that are offered under the Activities area. These lessons provide a solid foundation by covering both fundamental and complex ideas.

- **Use aid Options:** To make controls simpler and easier to understand while learning the ropes, activate aid options from the Options menu. Turn these tools off as you become better.
- **Free Flight on the World Map:** Take control of this playground as an aspiring pilot. To get a sense of what this simulator can provide, try out various aircraft, locations, and weather conditions.
- **Join the Community:** You may get insightful advice, helpful hints, and inspiration for your virtual aviation experiences by interacting with the enthusiastic flight simulation community.
- **Examine the Add-Ons:** Although Marketplace offers a lot, try to limit yourself to the essentials that you find appealing. For others, the experience is completed with extras like luxurious planes and scenery from your preferred areas.

CHAPTER TWO
CONFIGURING YOUR CONTROLS

Selecting the Best Control Configurations

To start configuring your controls, launch MSFS 2024 and choose the main menu. Click "Settings" in the upper right corner, and then choose "Controls." Keyboards, mouse, joysticks, and other controllers that are connected to your computer will all be shown on the left side of this interface. Make sure the simulator recognizes and connects to your preferred controller.

Comprehending Control Profiles

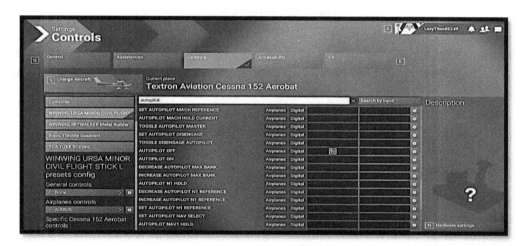

Three main categories comprise the hierarchical control profile system that MSFS 2024 has introduced:

+ **General Controls:** All aircraft and situations use the same keybindings. Camera controls, pause commands, and other standard simulator functions would fall under this category.

+ **Aircraft Category Controls:** These would comprise the key bindings associated with a certain aircraft category. Gliders, helicopters, and aircraft are a few examples. For fixed-wing and rotary-wing aircraft, you may wish to configure separate controls.

+ **Control for Specific Aircraft kinds:** These are exclusive to certain kinds of aircraft. Because each aircraft have distinct systems and functions, you can have a Boeing 737 and a Cessna 172, each with its own set of control profiles.

14

You are able to customize any aircraft or category to your exact specifications thanks to this multi-layered structure.

How to Establish and Maintain Control Profiles

In order to modify a control profile:

- **Select the Controller:** Click on a controller from the list on the left side of the Controls menu.
- **Choose the Profile Type:** General Controls, Aircraft Category Controls, or a specific Aircraft Model is the options available at the bottom of the page.
- **Make a copy of the default profile:** It is preferable to make a copy of the default profile prior to modifying. Next to the profile name, click the gear icon, then choose "Duplicate." For easy recognition, give the new profile a relevant name.
- **Edit Bindings:** Click on an empty function bar and hit the button or key on your controller. You may also search for the function you want or browse through the categories in which you want to bind this or that function. If any of these buttons have already been assigned to another function, a conflict number will show up next to it in red. To further examine and modify the conflict in this instance, click the options button.
- **Adjust Sensitivity:** By choosing the "Hardware Settings" option on the right, you may fine-tune responsiveness by adjusting sensitivity curves, dead zones, and other factors using axis controls like throttle quadrants or a joystick.
- **Save and Apply:** Don't forget to save the profile after configuring the controls. To set this as the default setting for that specific aircraft or category type, click the gear icon and choose "Set as Default."

By doing this, you can make sure that your control setups are unique and configured for different kinds of aircraft.

Control Profile Management While Taking flight

The following techniques may be used to see and modify control settings at any point while in flight:

- **Pause Menu:** Press the "Esc" key to bring up the Pause menu, followed by "Settings" and "Controls."
- **Toolbar:** To access control settings, click the controller symbol in the in-flight toolbar.

Because of this adaptability, you may make changes in real time without ending your flying experience.

Advice on the Best Control Configurations

+ **Start with Defaults:** Common controllers are automatically assigned default profiles by MSFS 2024. Use these defaults as a starting point and adjust them to your tastes.
+ **Prevent Conflicts:** If you assign too many functions to a single button or key, it may cause unintended actions to be performed. To identify and resolve disputes, use the conflict indicator numbers.
+ **Test Your Settings:** To see how everything works, fly your model in a test flight after configuring the controls. This often aids in further performance-enhancing tweaks.
+ **Make a backup of your profiles**: Make regular backups of your customized profiles to guard against configuration loss in the event of upgrades or other system modifications.

Setting Up Yokes and Joysticks

The setup of a joystick or yoke in Microsoft Flight Simulator 2024 (MSFS 2024) becomes crucial for improving a responsive and immersive flying experience. **Here is a detailed procedure for successfully establishing controls:**

+ **Establish a Device Connection:**
  ➢ **Plug-In:** Before launching MSFS 2024, make sure your joystick or yoke is directly linked to your computer.
  ➢ **Install Drivers:** Although the majority of modern devices are plug-and-play, it's always a good idea to install the most recent drivers from the manufacturer's website for improved performance.
+ **Start the 2024 version of Microsoft Flight Simulator:**
  ➢ **Launch the game:** Open MSFS 2024, and then choose the main menu.
  ➢ **Options for access:** 'Options' and 'Controls' are the next steps in the controls setup menu.

- **Determine Your Device:**
  - ➢ **Device Detection:** MSFS 2024 need to recognize attached peripherals automatically.
  - ➢ **Choose Your Device:** Tabs for each connected device will show up in the Controls menu. Select the tab that corresponds to your yoke or joystick.
- **Establish Control Bindings:**
  - ➢ **Preset Profiles:** For common devices, MSFS 2024 often includes preset control profiles. Check them out to see if they meet your requirements.
  - ➢ Changing the Bindings
  - ➢ **View All Commands:** To assign the whole range of functions, choose the filter to display all commands.
  - ➢ 'Aileron Axis' may be clicked, followed by the relevant button or by moving the axis on your device.
  - ➢ Click 'Apply and Save' to verify the modifications once they have been allocated.
- **Modify the Sensitivity Configuration:**

  - ➢ To access sensitivity options, choose 'Sensitivity' from the Controls menu to modify your device's response.
  - ➢ **Modify Curves:** To achieve the required responsiveness and provide smoother control inputs during flight, modify the sensitivity curves.
  - ➢ **Test Adjustments:** To make sure the modifications live up to your expectations, test them in flight after making them.
- **Maintain and Save Profiles:**
  - ➢ **Create Profiles:** It could be a good idea to develop distinct control profiles for various aircraft types in order to meet their various control requirements.

- ➢ **Naming conventions:** Give each profile a descriptive name, such as "Single Engine Prop" or "Jet Aircraft," so you can tell which profile will load without actually loading it.
- ➢ **Changing Profiles:** Choose the appropriate profile for the aircraft you want to fly before each trip.
- ✦ **Examine Your Setup:**
  - ➢ **Pre-Flight Check:** Verify that all controls function as intended after loading a flight.
  - ➢ **Fine Tune:** Return to the Sensitivity settings and make further changes if any controls are excessively sensitive or unresponsive.

Adjusting the Rudder Pedals

To have strong yaw control when flying in Microsoft Flight Simulator 2024, you must calibrate your rudder pedals. Below is a list of the steps.

- ✦ **Install the most recent firmware and drivers:** Start by downloading and installing the most recent firmware and drivers for your particular model of rudder pedal from the manufacturer's website. It will ensure that it functions with the newest features and hotfixes in MSFS 2024.
- ✦ **Use Windows to calibrate:** Before attempting to adjust any parameters in the simulator, start by calibrating your rudder pedals using Windows. **To do this:**
  - ➢ To launch the Game Controllers window, enter Win + R, type joy.cpl, and then hit Enter.
  - ➢ From the list, choose your rudder pedals, and then click "Properties."
  - ➢ After selecting the "Settings" menu, choose "Calibrate."
  - ➢ Make sure the pedals record the whole range of motion by calibrating each axis according to the on-screen directions.
  - ➢ Lastly, check for appropriate responsiveness by testing the pedals in the "Test" tab.
- ✦ **Configure MSFS 2024 Controls**
  - ➢ Open the control settings in Microsoft Flight Simulator 2024.
  - ➢ Go to Controls Options under Options.
  - ➢ Draw attention to your rudder pedal gadget.
  - ➢ Correctly set up the Rudder axis assignment: Click on the designated rudder axis box (for instance, "Rudder Axis"), then adjust your pedals to allow the input to be recognized. Click "Search by Input," shift the pedals, and then apply the detected input to the rudder axis if it hasn't already been allocated.
  - ➢ Assign each to the appropriate axis and repeat for the left and right toe brakes.

Modify the Sensitivity Configuration: For greater control precision, sensitivity curves can be adjusted:

> Choose the rudder pedals from the "Controls options," then click "Sensitivity."
> **Modify the sensitivity curve to get a tailored or linear response:**
>   ✓ The pedal range responds similarly to a linear curve.
>   ✓ It is possible to establish custom curves that make the pedals more responsive at the extremes and less sensitive in the middle.

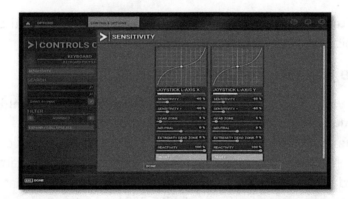

> Examine the response graph and compare the changes to your preferred flying style to see if they need any revisions.

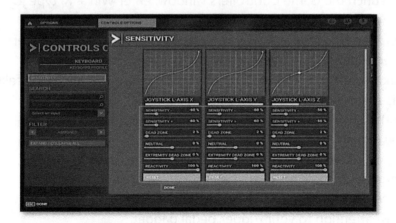

Flight Test: A test flight is carried out after calibration and setup to evaluate performance:

> To make sure differential braking is effective, taxi and engage the toe brakes.
> To ensure smooth, proportionate reaction and coordinate turns while in flight, employ the rudder.

Tips for Troubleshooting

+ Look for conflicting assignments if the rudder pedals are not working or are acting strangely. Make sure the identical controls aren't allocated to any other devices.
+ It may be necessary to remove and reinstall drivers for certain models before restoring the game controller's default settings.
+ Routinely ensure that your pedals are in excellent physical condition, all connections are secure, and moving components are well-lubricated.

Assigning Keyboard Shortcuts

Below is how one may create and change keyboard shortcuts:

Go to the Controls Settings

+ Open Microsoft Flight Simulator 2024 to start the simulator.
+ To access the Options, go to the main menu and choose "Options."
+ Select Controls Options: To see input devices, click "Controls Options".

Change or Assign Keyboard Shortcuts

+ Choose the Keyboard Profile: Click the keyboard in the device list under the "Controls Options" menu. A area for configuring keyboard presets is located on the bottom left. By default, the "Keyboard 2024 Transversal" profile is activated. To return to the more traditional MSFS 2020 shortcuts, click the arrow next to "Keyboard 2024 Transversal" and choose "Keyboard 2020."

+ **Locate a Specific Command:** Use the search box to locate the command you want to modify or reassign. To find the desired function, you may alternatively search via the categories.

- **Modify the Shortcut:** To make changes, click on the command. To assign a key, press the new key or key combination. Make sure the new task doesn't interfere with any shortcuts that are already in place.
- **Save Changes:** Click "Validate" to validate after assigning. Before leaving the menu, choose "Apply & Save" to ensure that all of the changes are applied.

Keeping Control Profiles Saved and Loaded

Consistency and efficiency are ensured by correctly storing and loading these profiles, particularly while using various devices or aircraft kinds.

Preserving Control Profiles

Use these procedures to save a control profile in MSFS 2024:
- Open Control Settings: Go to the main menu after starting MSFS 2024. Choose the "Controls" tab from the selections.
- Configure Controls: Choose your device (throttle quadrant, yoke, or joystick). Next, give buttons, axes, and switches the functionalities you want them to have.
- In order to save the profile, click "Save." Give it a distinctive profile name to prevent inadvertent overwriting by others. After that, make sure you are saving the profile by confirming the save.

Keep in mind that control profiles are saved in Microsoft's cloud together with your Xbox game profile in MSFS 2024. This implies that all of your settings are automatically backed up and restored between installations if you use the same profile.

Control Profiles for Loading

To load a control profile that has already been saved:
- Go to Control Settings: Navigate to the main menu after opening MSFS 2024. Choose "Options" and then "Controls."

- Choose the Device: Decide which device a profile needs to be loaded into.
- Click the "Load" button to load the profile. Select the profile you want to use from the list of stored profiles. Verify that the chosen profile will be applied.

Software defects or synchronization issues may cause custom profiles to not load or to return to their original settings. Eliminate the cloud save for these circumstances; doing so may fix either the crashing or the failure to load problems.

Control Profile Backup

Making a local backup is preferable, particularly for the Steam version, even if MSFS 2024 utilizes the cloud for control profiles.

Use these procedures to create a backup of your control profiles:
- **Find Profile Files:** Your Windows username is [YourUserName].
- **Copy Profile Files:** Open the "Controls" folder. Copy the XML files that represent your profiles.
- **Store Backups:** Place the duplicated data in a secure location, such a cloud storage service or external disk.

This allows you to restore your profiles and will act as a backup in the event of a system failure or reinstallation.

Typical Issues and How to Fix Them

In some cases, the control profiles may not load or store properly. Typical problems include:
- **Non-saving profiles:**
  - ➤ Verify that the game is authorized to write to the profile directory.
  - ➤ Look for patches or software upgrades that might address the identified problems.
- **Restoring Default Profiles:**
  - ➤ Prior to taking off, make sure the appropriate profile is chosen.
  - ➤ To see whether this resolves issues with loading and crashes, remove the cloud saves.

CHAPTER THREE
PERFORMANCE OPTIMIZATION AND GRAPHICS

Making Graphics Adjustments

Comprehending Graphics Configuration

There are several visual options in MSFS 2024, and each one has an impact on the simulation's appearance and functionality. The most crucial ones are:

- **Resolution:** This establishes the image's clarity. Sharper pictures are produced at higher resolutions, but the system demand increases.
- **Render Scaling:** This modifies the game's internal rendering resolution before resizing it to fit your screen. Performance may be enhanced by lowering this, but visual clarity may suffer.
- **Global Rendering Quality:** A mode that balances performance and aesthetics by adjusting many variables at once.
- **Object Level of Detail (OLOD) and Terrain Level of Detail (TLOD):** Manage the level of detail in objects and terrain. While higher numbers improve detail, they may also degrade performance.

- **Cloud Quality and Volumetric Clouds:** Although higher settings provide intricate clouds and may impact performance, cloud forms give the picture realism.

How to Adjust Graphics to Get the Best Results

- **Suggested Configuration:** By default, MSFS 2024 often chooses configurations that could be representative of your hardware. It may not always be the best arrangement for smoothness.
- **Modify the render scaling and resolution:**
  - ➢ **Resolution:** Try reducing the resolution if you're experiencing poor frame rates. For instance, performance will significantly improve when switching from 4K to 1440p.
  - ➢ **Render scale:** Performance is also impacted by adjusting render scale. Lowering it will result in a lower internal rendering resolution, which might boost frame rates at the expense of clarity.
- **Modify the quality of the global rendering:**
  - ➢ Select a lower default for Global Rendering Quality, such as Medium or Low, if performance is subpar.
  - ➢ As an alternative, you may manually tweak settings like Anti-Aliasing, Texture Quality, and Shadow Quality to help balance performance and aesthetics.
- **Optimization of Terrain Level of Detail (TLOD) and Object Level of Detail (OLOD):**
  - ➢ Performance may be enhanced by lowering TLOD and OLOD levels, particularly in crowded situations.
  - ➢ Generally speaking, values of around 200 are advised for a decent balance.
  - ➢ **Control Cloud Configuration:** Performance may be improved by lowering cloud quality and disabling volumetric clouds, although this may come at the expense of realistic cloud generation.
- **Turn off Superfluous Features:** It is possible to disable features like Motion Blur, Lens Flare, and Bloom, which will enhance functionality without changing the appearance.
- **Update your software and drivers:** To get the most recent updates and improvements, make sure your system software and graphics drivers are up to date.

About Testing

Once the modifications have been made, test the simulator in different situations to observe its performance. Keep an eye on visual quality, stuttering, and frame rates. Adjust parameters iteratively until your system is in the ideal equilibrium.

Configuring Display Preferences

Although Microsoft Flight Simulator 2024 (MSFS 2024) provides an engaging and breathtakingly beautiful experience, careful display setting modification is necessary to get the best possible visuals and performance. **High visual quality and fluid gameplay are guaranteed by proper setup.**

- **Render scaling and resolution:** Visual clarity is determined by display resolution, however internal rendering resolution is impacted by render scaling. Although they provide crisper pictures, higher resolutions and render scaling put greater strain on your machine. For example, using 100% render scaling and 3840x2160 (4K) resolution provides sharp images but may result in lower frame rates. However, if you want to get more speed out of it, consider lowering the resolution to 2560x1440 or using 80–90% render scaling. In return, it loses some detail texturing quality and doesn't suffer much from excessive framerate reduction.

- **Quality of Global Rendering:** A feature in MSFS 2024 called Global Rendering automatically modifies a number of graphics settings simultaneously. Although the highest settings, like Ultra, look amazing, they will strain your system's capabilities. Medium to High will work well for most systems in order to balance performance.

- **TLOD (Terrain Level of Detail) and OLOD (Object Level of Detail):** Terrain and object detail levels are controlled by TLOD and OLOD, respectively. While increasing values improves visual quality, performance suffers as a result. For example, frame rates may be poor with TLOD at 200 and OLOD at 100. Reducing them to 100 and 50, respectively, can result in a higher performance reward without significantly sacrificing aesthetics. Adapt these parameters to the performance of your gear.

- **Shadow and Cloud Configurations:** Clouds and shadows have a big effect on performance. Setting the cloud quality to Ultra and the shadow quality to High is a must. Lower the cloud and shadow quality to Medium or Low for improved performance without significantly sacrificing aesthetic appeal. You may play around with these parameters to see what works best for you.

- **Ambient Occlusion and Anti-Aliasing:** Ambient occlusion gives scenes depth, while anti-aliasing smoothes down sharp edges. Although they improve visual quality, certain features may have an impact on performance. A decent compromise between performance and aesthetics might be achieved by using TAA and adjusting ambient occlusion to Medium or Low. Adapt these parameters to the capability of your machine.
- **Frame Rate Limiter with V-Sync:** V-Sync synchronizes the frame rate with the refresh rate of your display. Although it may be used to stop screen tearing, V-Sync is often linked to input latency. V-Sync or a frame rate limiter, which caps your frame rate at your monitor's refresh rate for a much smoother experience without taxing your system, should be enabled if you are experiencing tearing.
- **Hardware Points to Remember:** The hardware of your machine determines the ideal settings. Users with high-end GPUs, such as the RTX 4080, may be able to outperform those with mid-range GPUs at higher settings. To get the greatest performance, you must adjust the parameters to the capability of your device.
- **Data Management and Streaming:** In order to display the globe, MSFS 2024 sends data in real time. You need a steady and fast internet connection for seamless streaming. To improve performance, control the rolling cache. To prevent performance degradation over time, make sure the cache has adequate disk space and make an effort to clear it off often.

Controlling Frame Rates

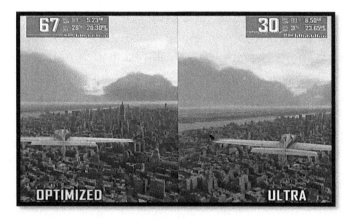

The amount of pictures your computer can generate in a second is known as its frame rate. While a lower FPS results in stuttering and a less engaging experience, a higher FPS rate helps things operate more smoothly. Frame constancy is crucial in MSFS 2024, particularly in intricate settings like cityscapes or intricately designed airports.

Enhancing Graphics Configuration

Using the in-game graphics options is one of the greatest methods to control frame rates. Here are a few important settings:

- **Resolution:** Reducing a game's resolution may have significant benefits. For instance, lowering the resolution from 4K to 1440p or 1080p often results in better frames per second. Finding a balance that suits you is crucial since this will impact visual quality.
- The basic solution that the game produces internally before scaling it to your native resolution is determined by render scaling. Higher frame rates may be achieved with lower render scaling, but the picture may become fuzzy. To discover the ideal balance for your system, change this parameter.
- **Global Rendering Quality:** There are many settings in MSFS 2024, including Low, Medium, High, and Ultra. Performance will be enhanced by lowering this option, but graphic quality may suffer. Try out several settings to get the ideal balance between aesthetics and performance.
- **Advanced Settings:** You may deactivate Terrain Level of Detail, Object Level of Detail, and Volumetric Clouds. Performance will be enhanced by doing this, especially in densely populated regions. Setting the TLOD to 200 and the OLOD to 100 would be a decent compromise.

Hardware Points to Remember

Your computer's hardware has a big impact on frame rate performance. The crucial elements to take into account are as follows:

- **Graphics Card (GPU):** To produce high-quality images, a strong GPU is required. Switching to a more powerful GPU will result in a noticeable improvement in performance if your frame rate is poor. For instance, adjusting parameters like Dynamic Super Resolution may improve performance for GPU owners like the NVIDIA RTX 4060 Ti.
- **Processor:** MSFS 2024 relies heavily on the CPU; the more CPU power, the more fluid the image will be during intricate simulations and visualizations. Getting a better CPU should help keep frame rates under control.
- **Memory (RAM):** A gamer may play games without jittering if they have the proper quantity of RAM. 32GB or more is necessary for a smooth experience, particularly when gamers are using other apps concurrently, even if 16GB would often fine.

Using Technologies to Improve Performance

The following technologies may improve the performance of modern GPUs:
- **NVIDIA DLSS (Deep Learning Super Sampling):** This technique upscales an inherently low-resolution picture using AI super-sampling methods, allowing for faster frame rates with no discernible quality loss. Frame rates are increased by switching from balanced mode to Performance mode.
- As with DLSS, AMD FidelityFX Super Resolution (FSR) upscales lower-resolution pictures to higher resolutions for better performance. Smoother gameplay may be achieved by using FSR, especially on AMD GPUs.

Aspects of the Network

MSFS 2024 uses streaming data to provide real-time weather, traffic, and landscape updates. A steady and quick internet connection is essential:
- **Internet Speed:** For optimal performance, it is advised that the connection speed be at least 50 Mbps. Slower connections may take longer to load new scenery or create stuttering.
- **Connection Stability:** To prevent interference when flying, make sure your connection is steady. Wi-Fi may not always be as dependable as a cable connection.

Extra Advice

- **V-Sync and Frame Rate Limiting:** While turning on V-Sync helps stop screen tearing, it may also limit your frame rate. As an alternative, frame rate limitation may provide steady performance.
- **Background Apps:** To free up system resources and enable MSFS 2024 to make greater use of your computer's capabilities, shut off any background apps that aren't needed.
- **Frequent Updates:** To take advantage of performance enhancements and bug fixes, keep your graphics drivers and the game itself updated.

Making Use of Performance Monitoring Instruments

Performance monitoring tools are operational on MSFS 2024 to provide useful information about current frame rates and CPU/GPU utilization in real time. To assess system performance while in flight, you might use the Ctrl + Shift + O key sequence to activate a small overlay that displays all of this information. These will enable you to quickly adjust settings to maintain performance and aesthetic smoothness.

Tools for Third-Party Performance Monitoring

Third-party tools are available to provide more insightful information and to elaborate with more accurate analyses:

 + **MSI Afterburner and Rivatuner Statistics Server (RTSS):** These two can operate in tandem, allowing for comprehensive on-GPU activity monitoring that includes temperatures and statistics. Additionally, on-screen representation of these metrics during flight can function as an effective in-flight performance observer.

 + **AMD Radeon Software:** The Radeon Software package for AMD GPU users offers performance monitoring tools that provide real-time analytics including frame rates, GPU utilization, and temperatures. These may be accessed and utilized to alter the parameters for the best possible performance.

 + **NVIDIA GeForce Experience:** The Geforce Experience app, available to owners of the NVIDIA series, provides performance monitoring tools that display parameters in real-time, including temperatures, usage, and frame rates. Setting changes to achieve peak performance is made easier with the help of these tools.

Monitoring of Network Performance

Network performance is monitored since MSFS 2024 requires streams of data for its expansive open environment.

 + **WinMTR:** This free Windows utility combines ping and traceroute to identify network problems that can be affecting MSFS 2024 streaming performance. In order to identify performance problems relating to the network, the user will be able to ascertain if there is delay or packet loss.

Using Performance Information to Adjust

The following actions may be taken to optimize MSFS 2024 settings once performance data has been collected:

 + **Modify Graphics parameters:** To improve frame rates, tone down parameters such as Texture Resolution, Shadow Quality, Anti-Aliasing, and many more based on performance indicators. For instance, lowering texture resolution may lead to significant speed improvements with little quality degradation.

 + **Control Background Processes:** To free up resources for MSFS 2024, launch performance monitoring tools to keep an eye on and terminate any unnecessary background programs that could be using up CPU and RAM.

 + **Network Settings Improvement:** When network performance is identified as a bottleneck, WinMTR and other tools may be used to identify and address problems with excessive latency or packet loss that may affect MSFS 2024 streaming performance.

Solving Typical Graphics Problems

Microsoft Flight Simulator 2024 (MSFS 2024) has received praise for its immersive experience and breathtaking visuals. Nevertheless, some users have had problems with the visuals, which might make it less enjoyable. **The instructions listed below provide helpful troubleshooting techniques for typical MSFS 2024 graphics issues.**

- **Update your graphics drivers:** Visual problems sometimes arise from outdated or faulty graphics drivers. To guarantee peak performance:
  - **Determine the Graphics Card You Have:**
    - ✓ Type dxdiag using Win + R, then hit Enter.
    - ✓ To get information on your graphics card, choose the "Display" tab in the DirectX Diagnostic tool.
  - **Get the Most Recent Drivers:**
    - ✓ Go to the official website of the company that makes your graphics card, such as AMD, Intel, or NVIDIA.
    - ✓ Install the most recent drivers that are compatible with your system after downloading them.
    - ✓ To implement the modifications, restart your computer when the installation is complete.
- **Modify the graphics settings in the game:** Excessive graphics settings might ultimately create poor system performance by bottlenecking your machine. **To optimize settings, follow these steps:**
  - To access the Graphics Settings, launch MSFS 2024 and choose the "Options" menu. Select "Graphics" to see the available options.
  - Modify Preferences: Disable options such as "Render Scaling," "Terrain Level of Detail," and "Object Level of Detail."
  - Disable or reduce "Anti-Aliasing" and "Ambient Occlusion," if at all feasible.
  - Try adjusting these parameters to achieve a decent balance between performance and appearance.
- **Look for Any Lost Game Files:** Game files that are missing or damaged may also create visual irregularities.
  - To confirm and fix, follow these steps:
  - **Version of the Microsoft Store:**
    - ✓ Launch the app for the Microsoft Store.
    - ✓ Select "Library" and then "Microsoft Flight Simulator."
    - ✓ Then choose "Manage" and finally "Repair."

- ➤ **Version on Steam:**
  - ✓ Go to your Library after launching Steam.
  - ✓ Take "Microsoft Flight Simulator" with a right-click, then choose "Properties."
  - ✓ Click "Verify Integrity of Game Files" under the "Local Files" tab to replace any corrupted files.
- ✦ **Keep an eye on the system temperature:** Graphical hiccups and crashes may result from overheating. **The following actions may be taken to keep an eye on and control temperatures:**
  - ➤ Use Monitoring Software: To monitor the GPU and CPU temperatures, use applications like HWMonitor or MSI Afterburner.
  - ➤ **Assure Adequate Cooling:**
    - ✓ Dust removal from heatsinks and fans
    - ✓ Make sure the space around your PC has enough ventilation.
    - ✓ If temperatures are very high, upgrade the cooling system.
    - ✓ This aids in keeping the system's temperature at ideal levels for operation.
- ✦ **Turn off background apps:** A game's performance may be impacted by other running apps using up system resources. In order to reduce interferences:
  - ➤ Close Superfluous applications: Before launching MSFS 2024, close any unnecessary applications, such as media players and web browsers.
  - ➤ Use Task Manager: Press Ctrl + Shift + Esc to launch the Task Manager. Programs that use excessive amounts of memory or CPU should be closed.
  - ➤ More resources are available for the game as a result.
- ✦ **Look for conflicts in the software:** Certain software may not work with MSFS 2024, particularly overlays and third-party apps.
  - ➤ **To identify and resolve conflicts:**
    - ✓ Disable Overlays: Turn off overlays from programs like NVIDIA GeForce Experience, Discord, and Steam for a while.
    - ✓ Uninstall Conflicting applications: To find the source of issues, try deleting recently installed applications if they continue.
    - ✓ Reinstalling MSFS 2024 could also fix issues.
- ✦ **Refresh DirectX:** Graphical problems may arise from an outdated version of DirectX. To provide an update:
  - ➤ **Get the most recent DirectX:**
    - ✓ Visit Microsoft DirectX's official download website.
    - ✓ Install the most recent version that is compatible with your system after downloading it.
    - ✓ Restart your computer when the installation is complete.

- **Modify the Virtual Memory Configuration:** The majority of computer issues are brought on by a shortage of virtual memory. To adapt:
  - ➢ **Modify the virtual memory:**
    - ✓ Click "System," then "Control Panel," and then "Advanced system settings."
    - ✓ Select "Settings" from the "Advanced" tab's "Performance."
    - ✓ Under the "Virtual memory" section of the "Advanced" menu, choose "Change."
    - ✓ Configure a custom size whose beginning and maximum values match the RAM of your machine.
    - ✓ This guarantees the game has enough virtual memory.
- **Install MSFS 2024 again:** If problems continue, a new installation could be required:
  - ➢ **Uninstall the game:** Go to your system settings and follow the normal uninstall procedure.
  - ➢ **Reinstall:** Get MSFS 2024 from the official website and install it.

CHAPTER FOUR
EXPLORING THE MAP OF THE WORLD

Investigating the World

Earth's Digital Twin

Building a "digital twin" of Earth is the fundamental idea of MSFS 2024. This enormous project uses cutting-edge technology to meticulously replicate Earth's cities, landscapes, and natural marvels. It combines procedural generating methods with high-resolution pictures to provide an unmatched level of quality and immersion.

Improved Flight Planning and World Map

The quality of MSFS 2024's globe map has been increased, making ground planning easier. Both IFR and VFR map layers, which include extensive charts and route planning capabilities, are supported by new flight planners. It is now possible to prepare in great detail for everything from intercontinental trips to local regional flights.

Beyond Exploring the Cockpit

The opportunity to exit your aircraft and visit the surrounding surroundings is one feature that sets MSFS 2024 apart. In a manner similar to virtual tourism, the software's invention allows users to enter the virtual world and see cities, monuments, and natural marvels. It goes into great depth on everything from peacefully trekking through the Swiss Alps to strolling through the bustling streets of New York City.

Different Biomes and Interest Areas

With hundreds of plant species and dynamically created elements like grass, pebbles, and flowers, MSFS 2024 provides 27 intricately designed biomes. These biomes shift in response to seasonal weather cycles, which alters the terrain's general appearance and structure. The simulator offers users virtual touring at over 2,000 areas of interest, including well-known landmarks and natural marvels.

Maritime Traffic and Wildlife

By include a wide variety of land-based creatures in their native environments and freely roaming cattle from all over the world, the simulator makes the planet come to life. Large tankers, cargo ships, trawlers, and tugs are all part of the dynamic, global maritime traffic that fills the oceans and rivers. Because of this dynamic environment, the simulation is more realistic and every flight is a different experience.

Career Mode and Activities under Guidance

Users may choose from a variety of aviation vocations in MSFS 2024's expanded career mode, including search and rescue work and commercial piloting. It gives pilots a feeling of purpose and accomplishment and provides well-structured advancement via missions and difficulties. Pilots of all skill levels will also enjoy a variety of thrilling experiences via guided activities such as pinpoint landings, rally races, and low-altitude trials.

Mode of the Photographer

For those who want to capture the beauty of the virtual environment, MSFS 2024 offers the Photographer Mode. Traveling throughout the world allows one to see well-known sites, take in the stunning natural scenery, and record these experiences with photographs in a travel journal. Special picture challenges put your artistic vision and flying prowess to the test as you attempt to capture the ideal moment.

Atmospheric effects and weather that is realistic

With the addition of additional cloud types, auroras, and other weather events, MSFS 2024 increases atmospheric and weather realism. The environment seems much more realistic than ever thanks to the entirely revamped photometric lighting system. Engaging, dynamic flying experience.

International Society and Occurrences

With events like its flagship Community Fly-in Friday, which takes place every Friday at 11:00 am Pacific Time (19:00 UTC), anyone can fly into an open event that is open to all pilots, regardless of skill level, just to have fun, try something new, or meet new people. This furthers the simulator's mission of creating a vibrant global community.

Designing a Flight Route

Here are some tips for using a global map to direct your next journey:
- **Go to the Flight Planner**
  - ➢ Accessing the MSFS 2024 flight planning user interface from the simulator's main menu is simple.
  - ➢ Launch the "World Map" after opening the simulator. A global map appears, allowing one to customize their itinerary, add waypoints, and choose their airports of departure and arrival.

- **Choosing Airports for Arrivals and Departures:** At the airport of departure of your choice, click on the global map. 'Set as departing' will be an option on the menu that appears. Choose your destination airport in the same way after that.

35

Because MSFS 2024 has so many airports throughout the globe, you should be able to arrange flights from and to almost anyplace.

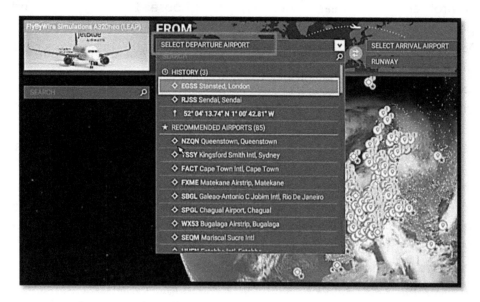

- **Select the Type of Flight Plan:** Select the kind of flight plan you want to create:
  - ➢ Pilots who like to fly with visual aids would benefit greatly from the Visual Flight Rules (VFR).
  - ➢ **Instrument Flight Rules (IFR):** These are beneficial for anyone who wants to fly using instruments, usually in bad weather.
  - ➢ Selecting the appropriate flight plan type is essential since it will also dictate the aircraft's path and airways.
- **Make use of the flight planner online:** Working Title has released new web-based companion software for MSFS 2024 that will facilitate the creation and sharing of flight plans. Launch planner.flightsimulator.com, and then sign in with your Xbox login credentials. This platform allows you to plan comprehensive flights including airways, procedures, and waypoints, which you can then share with your buddies for multiplayer flying.
- **Including Airways and Waypoints:** Now that you have established your starting and ending sites, you may enhance your route by adding waypoints. To add waypoints, click on the map or use the search button to locate particular locations. In order to make navigation even easier, MSFS 2024 does support airways, which are pre-established pathways in the sky. Select an airway from the list that appears after clicking on the route line.

- **Including STARs and SIDs:** Predetermined routes known as Standard Instrument Departures (SIDs) and Standard Terminal Arrival Routes (STARs) are used to control air traffic near major airports. Choose the departure and arrival procedures from the list of possibilities to include them into your flight plan. Make sure the adjustments match your desired path since choosing a SID or STAR may cause your route to vary.
- **Examine the flight plan and save it:** Check your route for accuracy when it's finished. Look for any routing faults or discontinuities. The "Route Review" tool in MSFS 2024 identifies possible problems. Click the "Save Flight Plan" button to save the plan when it has been verified. After that, you can give your idea a name and decide whether or not to share it with others.
- **Bringing the Simulator's Flight Plan in:** Just starts a Free Flight session to use your stored flight plan in the simulator. Open your EFB and choose "Load Flight Plan." Then, from the list, choose your stored plan and load it into the simulator. To fully incorporate the plan into the simulator's systems, be sure to click the "File Plan with ATC" and "Send Route to Avionics" buttons.
- **Final Setup:** Verify that the weather, time of day, and aircraft are all adjusted to your liking before you take off. There is real-time weather in MSFS 2024. During your flight, you may experience the same weather conditions as any other location in the actual world at that very time.

Choosing Airports for Arrivals and Departures

To configure departure and arrival airports, follow these steps:
- **Launch the World Map:** Click the World Map button once MSFS 2024 has launched. The whole planet, its airports, and a few waypoints are visible here.
- Click the "Departure" section at the top of the page to choose the departure airport. There will be a search bar. Enter the airport's name or the ICAO, such as "EGLL" for London Heathrow. Then, from the search results, choose the airport of your choice.
- **Choosing the Arrival Airport:** Next to the Departure field is the "Arrival" field. Press it. To choose your destination airport, repeat the previous search procedure.
- **Route Planning:** Click the "Find Route" option after choosing both airports. A flight plan including the route, waypoints, and airways will be generated by the simulator.
- **Pick Procedures:** Click each block to pick the SIDs and STARs, respectively, if you want to operate under IFR. These charts are not available at every airport. It is

quite likely that a small field would not have any published SIDs or STARs that could continue to fly on VFRs.

- **Improve Your Flight Plan:** Verify the final route to make sure it is accurate and comprehensive. Make any required adjustments to processes or waypoints. Click "Fly" to begin your flight when you are satisfied with your flight plan.

Other Things to Think About

- **Flight Planning Tools:** Little Navmap and SimBrief are two examples of external flight planning tools that MSFS 2024 supports. Detailed flight plans may be made with the use of these tools and then transferred into the simulator.
- **Planes Restrictions:** specific procedures are not supported by specific planes. For instance, certain airports do not allow the Beechcraft King Air 350 to pick particular arrival or departure protocols.
- **User Interface:** The departure option dropdown list is updated with a list of often used airports via the World Map interface. This list may not always include the airport where you last arrived since it is based on your most recent departures.
- **Flight Plan Import:** Make sure the external application you use for flight planning generates a flight plan that works with MSFS 2024. Some players are currently having trouble importing an IFR flight plan into the EFB in-game.
- **System Updates:** Your installation of MSFS 2024 should be up to date for the newest features and bug patches, since older versions have certain flaws that haven't been fixed yet, which can hinder the flight planning stage.

Comprehending Weather Conditions

Custom weather versus live weather

There are two main weather modes offered by MSFS 2024:

- **Live Weather:** This mode updates in real-time to reflect current atmospheric occurrences worldwide, simulating actual weather conditions. For anyone looking for real flying experiences, it's perfect.
- **Custom Weather:** This option lets you manually change weather settings so you may practice in different situations or replicate certain scenarios.

Getting to and Changing Weather Preferences

Prior to takeoff:

- **Launch Free Flight:** Select "Free Flight" from the main menu to launch the globe map.
- **Modify Flight Conditions:** Click the "Flight Conditions" panel, which is often located in the upper right corner of the globe map.
- Select the "Weather" option to select the weather mode. "Live" or "Custom" weather options are available.

- **Modify Weather (if applicable): If you choose "Custom," you may change the following parameters:**
  - **Cloud Coverage:** Modify the kind and quantity of clouds.
  - **Precipitation:** Choose whether it will rain or snow, as well as its severity.
  - **Wind:** Adjust the direction and speed of the wind at various elevations.
  - **Temperature:** Adjust temperatures at different altitudes.
  - **Pressure:** Modify the parameters for atmospheric pressure.
  - **Save Settings:** To apply the weather conditions you have configured for your flight, save the settings.

While in flight:
- To activate the in-flight menu, move your mouse pointer to the top of the screen and choose it.
- Click the cloud symbol to access Weather Settings.
- Modify the Weather: You may modify the weather conditions while in flight. However, there are a few small performance hiccups while the simulation refreshes if you make drastic adjustments.

Advanced Weather Functions

The following are a few of the cutting-edge features included in MSFS 2024:
- **Aurora Borealis:** During certain times and places, the Northern Lights may be seen, giving flights over high-latitude regions a distinctive visual viewpoint.
- **Dynamic Weather Phenomena:** This simulator incorporates new weather phenomena, such changes in cloud and precipitation kinds, to make the experience more realistic.

Flight Plans: Saving and Loading

Preserving Flight Schedules

Use these procedures to save a flight plan in MSFS 2024:
- To access the flight planner, choose the flight planning option from the main menu.
- Make Your Flight Plan: To map your flight path, enter your destination and arrival airports as well as any waypoints you may have.
- Save the Plan: Select the Save option when your plan is finished. The term 'Save' or a disk icon should be used to symbolize it. To save your flight plan, click here. After that, you'll be asked to provide the file name and location for storage.

The majority of stored flight plans are typically in the.pln file type, which you may load into the simulator at any time.

Flight Plans Loading

To load a flight plan that has already been stored, follow these steps:

- **Launch Flight Planner:** From the main menu, launch the flight planning section.
- **Load the Plan:** Click the load option, which is often shown by an open folder icon or labeled "Load." Then, locate your.pln file, choose it, and make sure.

- **Review and Modify:** After loading, check that the flight plan is configured properly. Before continuing, make any necessary adjustments.

Your route, waypoints, and other characteristics are set up when you load a flight plan so that you may begin flying using the pre-established data.

Saving Flights in Progress and Loading Them

A user may pause and restart a flight at any moment since MSFS 2024 permits the saving and loading of flights that are currently in process. **The steps involved in saving an ongoing flight are as follows:**

- Press the Pause button to halt the flight, which will bring the simulation to an end.
- The 'Tab' key is used to access the Electronic Flight Bag (EFB).
- Save the Flight: Select 'LOAD/SAVE PLN FILE' after opening the EFB. You may save your flight in progress as a.flt file by putting down the chosen filename with the.flt extension, even if the UI suggests saving.pln files. This preserves your flight's current condition.

To load a flight that has been stored in progress:

- Launch a New Flight: Launch a new flight from the main menu.
- The EFB may be accessed by using the 'Tab' key.
- Load the Flight: Click 'LOAD FROM THIS PC' under the 'LOAD/SAVE PLN FILE' area. Then, use the file dialog to locate and choose your saved.flt file. You may need to put *.* in the filename field to show all file types in order to view.flt files, since the file dialog may default to displaying.pln files.

⊥ Resuming the Flight: You may use the stored state to restart your flight after loading.

It's crucial to remember that the ability to save and load flights that are already in progress may have restrictions or call for certain actions in order to perform properly. This function may not be completely implemented in all situations, and users have reported having varied experiences with it.

Other Things to Think About

⊥ **File Types:** In-progress flights are kept in.flt format, while flight plans are recorded in.pln format. Remember that in order to prevent incompatibilities, you should load and save file types correctly.

⊥ **EFB Usage:** For handling flight plans and ongoing flights, the Electronic Flight Bag (EFB) is a crucial instrument. To get the most of these capabilities, be sure to familiarize yourself with its interface.

CHAPTER FIVE
CHOOSING AND CUSTOMIZING AIRCRAFTS
Looking Through the Available Aircraft

The World Map interface, which serves as the primary gateway for flight planning, is shown to you as MSFS 2024 starts. Typically located toward the bottom of the screen, choose the 'Aircraft Selection' option first. This brings up a menu with every aircraft type accessible, arranged as follows: military, commercial, and general aviation. There are now further divisions into more focused areas within each category. One excellent illustration of this is the category of General Aviation, which encompasses Single-Engine Piston, Multi-Engine Piston, and Turboprop aircraft. Because of this tree structure, it's easy to browse through and quickly identify the aircraft that best suits your demands or flying assignment. MSFS 2024 provides comprehensive information on each aircraft to aid in your decision-making. A quick summary of the model, manufacturer, and a brief description appears when you hover over the symbol of an aircraft. Selecting an aircraft displays a more comprehensive profile with high-resolution photos, performance information, and specs. This guarantees that you may choose according to your flying objectives and degree of expertise.

Customization of Aircraft

By enabling you to customize different parts of your aircraft, MSFS 2024 expands the personalization experience. **After choosing your preferred aircraft, you may access a customization menu where you can change parameters like:**

- **Aircraft Registration:** To make your aircraft unique, tail numbers it. Pilots of virtual airlines and users who like flying around with individual touches in every area of the simulator are quite happy with this choice. Some players complained that the game arbitrarily assigned tail numbers based on the selected nation, disregarding their own registration choice. Future patches and upgrades may need to improve this feature.
- **Selection of Liveries:** There will be a variety of basic, personalized, and community-generated designs available. This will make your aircraft more aesthetically pleasing by allowing you to fly in the colors of your preferred airlines or distinctive personalized designs.
- **Flight Plan and Route:** By selecting the airports of departure and arrival, waypoints, and airways, you may design your flight plan. Planning itineraries of

any length, from a quick regional flight to a lengthy international trip, requires careful consideration of this.

- ✦ **Weather and Time Settings:** For various flying situations, adjust the weather, season, and time of day. This allows you to practice flying in poor visibility situations, such as thunderstorms.
- ✦ **Aircraft Configuration:** To replicate various operating conditions, alter variables such as fuel load, payload, and cargo. It is helpful if you are interested in the logistical aspects of flying or wants to train on an aircraft for certain tasks.

By using the 'Customize' button on the World Map interface; you can modify these settings within each aircraft profile from the interface you're using. This makes every flight customized to the precise setting you want and enhances your realistic simulation experience.

Comparing the Specifications of Different Aircraft

Comparing the various MSFS 2024 aircraft classes:

Commercial Aircraft

Within MSFS 2024, there are a few commercial aircraft designed to meet certain operating requirements. These consist of:

- ✦ **Airbus A320 NEO v2:** An improvement on the already well-liked A320 family, the NEO series A320 has improved avionics and fuel efficiency, making it an ideal option for short- to medium-distance flights.
- ✦ **Airbus A321LR:** This A320 family member's long-range sibling, the Airbus A321LR, can fly for considerably longer on transcontinental flights.
- ✦ **Airbus A330 Series:** The A330 series consists of aircraft like the A330-800 and A330-900, which are renowned for their extended range and roomy cabins that can accommodate both passengers and cargo.
- ✦ **Boeing 747-8:** The 747-8 is a long-haul, wide-body aircraft that is widely used for international flights and is noted for its huge capacity.
- ✦ **Boeing 737 MAX:** The 737 MAX series is a well-liked option for short- to medium-haul flights because to its enhanced fuel economy and cutting-edge technology.
- ✦ **Boeing 787-10:** A Dreamliner derivative, the 787-10 offers improved passenger comfort and fuel economy for medium-to long-haul flights.

Aircraft for General Aviation

MSFS 2024 offers a range of aircraft for aficionados of general aviation, including:

- **Cessna 172 Skyhawk (G1000):** This multipurpose single-engine aircraft is used for both training and leisure flights.
- **Cirrus SR22:** This high-performance single-engine aircraft is ideal for cross-country travel and is renowned for its pure speed and cutting-edge avionics.
- **Diamond DA40 NG:** This contemporary single-engine aircraft has cutting-edge avionics and exceptional fuel economy.
- **Pilatus PC-12 NGX:** This aircraft combines the comfort and travel capabilities of a light jet with the mission flexibility of a single-engine turboprop.
- **Beechcraft King Air 350i:** One of the most well-liked and dependable aircraft for freight and passenger transportation is the twin-turboprop King Air 350i.

Helicopters

Additionally, MSFS 2024 has a number of helicopters planned to demonstrate your abilities:

- **Airbus H125:** This single-engine helicopter may be used for a variety of tasks, including aerial work and search and rescue.
- **Airbus H225:** Among its many uses, the H225 is a twin-engine helicopter intended for long-distance flights and used for offshore transportation.
- **Boeing CH-47D Chinook:** This tandem-rotor helicopter is designed for heavy-lift transportation and is often used to deliver huge cargo.
- **Robinson RS6:** This lightweight, single-engine helicopter is ideal for training and light utility tasks due to its exceptional agility.

Amphibious Aircraft

MSFS 2024 has amphibious planes for water landings:

- **Dornier Seastar:** This amphibious aircraft can operate both on land and in the water and is capable of flying in a variety of settings.
- **Albatross G111:** This twin-engine amphibious aircraft, which can fly from land or the sea, is used for surveillance and cargo operations.

Personalization Choices

MSFS 2024 offers a wide range of aircraft modification possibilities, including:

- **Avionics and Instrumentation:** To meet certain operational requirements, pilots may alter avionics suites, which include GPS units, autopilot settings, and flight management systems.

- **Exterior and Interior Modifications:** Options include changing the cabin arrangement to make it more aesthetically and operationally pleasant, as well as adding new paint jobs and decals.
- **Performance tuning:** To make an aircraft more suited for a certain mission or set of flying circumstances, adjustments may be made to the engine's performance, the weight distribution of the aircraft, and the aerodynamics.

Personalizing Liveries

In MSFS 2024, liveries are designs that are applied to aircraft and consist of various graphical elements like as paint schemes and logos. Two primary categories of liveries exist:

- The aircraft model includes permanent designs known as static liveries. They are made according to the aircraft, and the colors are specified in the materials and textures. Static liveries lack the versatility of dynamic customization, while being quite simple to construct.
- **Dynamic Liveries:** These are made to either be modifiable by the user or to change on their own throughout the simulation under certain circumstances. These often depend on the simulator to dynamically alter colors and patterns, with all of their textures in white. For instance, in career modes or missions where the aircraft appearances may vary depending on the scenario, this provides a much more realistic experience.

Customizing MSFS 2024 Liveries

Use these procedures to alter aircraft liveries in MSFS 2024:

- To see the aircraft configuration, launch the world map. To see every aircraft that is accessible, click the aircraft symbol in the upper left corner. After selecting your preferred aircraft, click "Configure." You will be able to alter the livery once you are in the configuration screen.

- **Pick a Livery:** You may choose from the options in the liveries area. Select your preferred livery. Verify that you will be using the livery on your aircraft.
- **Installing Custom Liveries:** Download custom liveries from Flightsimto and other reliable sources. After downloading the files, extract them and place them in the "Community" folder of the MSFS 2024 directory that you installed. To make sure the updated liveries are detected, restart the simulator.

Making Your Own Liveries

For those who want to design their own liveries:

- **Resources and Tools:**
  - The MSFS 2024 Software Development Kit should be used. This will include all the necessary tools and documentation for creating liveries.
  - Learn how to create textures using image editing programs like Adobe Photoshop or GIMP.
- **The design process**
  - Create a template or use the basic textures of the aircraft.
  - When designing your livery, make sure it complies with the aircraft's model specs.
  - Verify the livery's correctness and aesthetic appeal on the simulator.

Establishing Weight and Fuel Parameters

Getting into the Performance Settings of the Aircraft

In MSFS 2024, use the Electronic Flight Bag (EFB) included into the simulator to change the fuel and weight settings:

- Click the airplane symbol at the bottom of the EFB interface to open the EFB.
- Go to Performance Settings: Choose "Flight Performance" from the EFB's menu.
- Modify Mass and Balance: To see specific settings, click the gear icon in the "Mass and Balance" section.

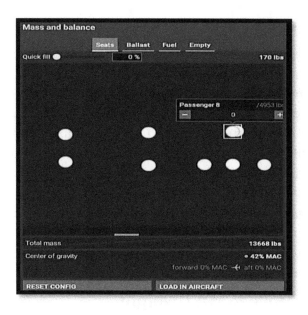

Fuel Parameter Setting

The fuel parameters may be adjusted under the "Mass and Balance" section:

* **Gasoline Quantity:** By entering the desired gasoline quantity in gallons or liters, you may alter the overall fuel load.
* **Individual Tank Fuel Levels:** To properly distribute the weight of an airplane with several fuel tanks, you may adjust the fuel amount for each tank independently.
* **Fuel Type:** Select between Jet-A and Avgas.
* Click "Load in aircraft" to put the gasoline into the aircraft once you've adjusted the parameters.

Changing the Weight Parameters

For the aircraft to operate safely, weight adjustments are crucial for keeping the aircraft's CG within acceptable bounds. To do this,

- **Passengers and Seats:** Decide how many people are going as well as their respective weights.
- **Cargo:** You must enter the weight and location of the cargo items.
- The weights of the pilot and co-pilot shall be set at 170 pounds apiece, or any other specified operating weight.
- **Station Loads:** By defining their weight and location with relation to the aircraft's reference datum, additional stations for loads, such as luggage compartments may be added.

Make that the CG stays within the allowed ranges for safe operation and that the overall weight does not surpass the aircraft's MTOW.

Comprehending Balance and Weight

The arrangement of weight and balance affects the stability and control of an aircraft. The simulator in MSFS 2024 offers a number of tools for seeing and modifying the CG:

- **Weight Debug Window:** This tool shows the CG location and weight distribution of the aircraft.
- **Show Gizmo Option:** This feature helps with accurate weight distribution by enabling the visible positioning of fuel tanks and load stations within the simulator.

This will assist the aircraft avoid operating outside of its design envelope, which might lead to issues like nose or tail heaviness.

Changing the Default Payload and Fuel Values

In MSFS 2024, the following default fuel and payload quantities may be configured for certain aircraft:

- **Pre-Flight Setup:** Prior to a flight, use the menu to choose an aircraft.
- **Modify Loadout:** To adjust the appropriate fuel and cargo amounts, click the spinning wheel symbol.
- **Set as Default:** A lot of people have asked for the ability to set them as defaults for flights in the future. Although not accessible at the moment, it is nevertheless a popular subject among MSFS community members.

Comprehending Aircraft Types

There are many kinds of aircraft in MSFS 2024, each with a specific function and a range of flight experiences. These consist of:

- **GA, or general aviation:**
  - ➤ **Description:** Light, compact aircraft are mostly used for commercial, leisure, or individual travel.
  - ➤ The Diamond DA40 TDI, Beechcraft Baron G58, and Cessna 172 Skyhawk are a few examples.
  - ➤ **Customization:** The pilot has the freedom to alter interior layouts, paint jobs, and avionics as they see fit.
- **Commercial Aircraft:**
  - ➤ **Synopsis:** Larger aircraft carry passengers and cargo across short to long distances.
  - ➤ Airbus A320, Boeing 737 Max 8, and Airbus A400M are a few examples.
  - ➤ **Customization:** All internal settings and avionics are configured to reflect real-world configuration parameters; however external liveries may be changed.
- **Military Aircraft:**
  - ➤ **Description:** Aircraft used by the military, such as cargo aircraft, fighters, and bombers.
  - ➤ The F-22 Raptor and the A-10 Warthog are two examples.
  - ➤ **Customization:** This might include performance adjustments, camouflage patterns, and weapon load-outs.
- **The helicopter:**
  - ➤ **Description:** Suitable for a range of operations, rotary-wing aircraft can take off and land vertically.
  - ➤ The Bell 407 and the Airbus Helicopter H125 are two examples.
  - ➤ **Customization:** Pilots may modify external attachments, avionics, and rotor configurations.
- **Specialized aircraft:**
  - ➤ **Overview:** Contains unusual aircraft such as gliders, hot air balloons, and airships.
  - ➤ Airship Industries Airship and Hot Air Balloon are two examples.
  - ➤ **Customization:** Due to the specialized nature of these aircraft, there is little room for customization.

Customization of Aircraft in MSFS 2024

MSFS 2024 provides a sophisticated range of customization choices. It enables pilots to personalize their aircraft to suit their tastes:
- **Instruments and Avionics:**
  - **General Aviation:** GPS systems, autopilot settings, and instrument panels are all part of the avionics suites, which may be updated or modified.
  - **Military and commercial aircraft:** Liveries and small interior adjustments are the principal forms of personalization.
- **Interior and Exterior Design:**
  - **Paint Schemes:** In addition to custom-painted liveries, a variety of other liveries are available.
  - **Interior Configurations:** Mostly for general aviation aircraft, several adjustments may be made to the cockpit, seating arrangements, and cabin layout.
- **Optimizing Performance:**
  - **Engine Modifications:** To improve performance, certain aircraft might choose to update or modify their engines.
  - **Weight and Balance:** Pilots may influence aircraft performance and handling by modifying fuel distribution and payloads.

Getting to and Controlling Aircraft

In MSFS 2024, to access and control aircraft:
- **Choosing an Aircraft:**
  - To see a list of available aircraft arranged by aircraft type, use the aircraft selection menu.
  - To access the customization menu for any aircraft, click on it.
- **Interface for Customization:**
  - Click on the avionics, exterior, interior, and performance settings tabs once you're in a menu tailored to your aircraft.
  - Make the necessary adjustments and save the settings.
- **Conserve Custom Settings:**
  - Save the configuration after making changes to ensure that the settings are retained for next flights.

CHAPTER SIX

ABOUT PRE-FLIGHT TECHNIQUES

Performing an Inspection Prior to Flight

A pre-flight inspection is a thorough examination of the aircraft to make sure everything is in working condition and that there are no flaws. In MSFS 2024, this is made possible via interactive checklists and intricate airplane models that allow users to remove coverings, chocks, and pins and inspect the condition of various components.

Getting to the Checklist before Flight

Checklists are included into the Electronic Flight Bag (EFB) in MSFS 2024 in an effort to improve usability. To access the checklist for pre-flight:
- ⨅ To start the EFB, use the TAB key.
- ⨅ After selecting the aircraft symbol, choose "Checklist."

The pre-flight checklist will appear for you to complete as a result.

Conducting the Pre-Flight Assessment

In MSFS 2024, pre-flight inspection is carried out as realistically as feasible, and user input is necessary for the interactions.

The steps are as follows:
- **Take off the covers, pins, and shocks:**
  - ➢ To remove landing gear pins, engine covers, pitot tube covers, and static port covers, interact with the aircraft model.
  - ➢ To make sure the wheel chocks are removed for mobility, move the aircraft.
- **Physical and Visual Inspections:**
  - ➢ Examine the aircraft's appearance, paying particular attention to the wings, tail, and fuselage.
  - ➢ The appropriate movement of all control surfaces, such as rudders, elevators, and ailerons, must be examined.
  - ➢ Examine the landing gear, tires, and brakes.
- **Verify the levels of oil and fuel:**
  - ➢ There should be no pollution in the gasoline tanks, and they should be properly filled.
  - ➢ It is necessary to check the oil level and search for any leaks.
- **Examine the avionics and flight instruments:**
  - ➢ Every flight instrument has to be calibrated and operational.
  - ➢ To ensure all avionics systems are operating, make sure they are switched on.
  - ➢ **Examine the emergency supplies:** Check for the availability and condition of first-aid supplies, fire extinguishers, life jackets, etc.

Making Use of the Auto Checklist Function

To assist you with your pre-flight checks, MSFS 2024 uses an auto checklist tool. To make the automatic checklists active:
- To access your EFB, select "Checklist."
- Select "Auto Checklist" from the menu.
- Comply with the pre-flight inspection procedures by following the simulator's instructions.

Making Good Use of Checklists

Checklists in MSFS 2024 are arranged into phases, with many checks in each step. Among other flight stages, these actions correlate to pre-flight, before taxi, and before departure. Every checkpoint covers every job that has to be done in detail by combining a topic ("Parking brake") with an expectation ("Set"). Although most checklists are tailored to a given aircraft, they can come in a variety of forms to accommodate various tasks and setups.

Getting to and Using Checklists

Use the in-game tablet in MSFS 2024 to access checklists:
- To open the tablet, use the TAB key.
- Select the symbol of an airplane.
- Click the "Checklist" option on the menu.

This interface displays the checklist's pages, each of which corresponds to a distinct flying phase. How many of the checkpoints on the chosen page have been verified is shown by the "val/total" figures at the top.

Making Good Use of Checklists

In order to make the most of checklists in MSFS 2024:
- **Comply with the Checklist Flow:** Follow the procedures listed in the checklist exactly. By doing this, operational integrity is maintained and all required activities are completed in the right sequence.
- **Recognize Every Checkpoint:** Before beginning a work, be sure you understand its goal and its anticipated result. This information improves situational awareness and makes the encounter more engaging.
- **Make Use of Visual Aids:** MSFS 2024 incorporates visual aids into checklists, such as emphasizing pertinent systems or controls. These assist the user in appropriately locating and setting values.
- **Practice Often:** Using the checklists consistently throughout flights enables the user to gain proficiency and confidence, which results in more realistic and efficient operations.

The Best Ways to Make a Checklist

For anybody wishing to modify or create new checklists:
- **Examine Aircraft Procedures:** Find out the regular operating procedures for this aircraft by consulting the Pilot Operating Handbook (POH) and other reliable sources.
- **Checklists' logical structure:** Tasks should be arranged with distinct stages and checkpoints that correspond to the periods of flight.
- **Add Visual and automated elements:** To expand functionality and improve the checklist's user experience, make advantage of MSFS 2024's capabilities to add visual and automated elements.
- **Testing and Improvement:** To guarantee the checklist's effectiveness and precision, conduct test flights once it has been developed or altered. To increase its usefulness, get input and make the required modifications.

Configuring Instruments and Avionics

Avionics refers to the electronic systems that are utilized for flight management, navigation, and communication. In MSFS 2024, these systems have been meticulously and very realistically reproduced.

Important elements consist of:

- **Primary Flight Display (PFD):** direction, altitude, airspeed, and attitude.
- **Multi-Function Display (MFD):** weather radar, navigation map, and more auxiliary information.
- **Flight Management System (FMS):** Facilitates autopilot integration, performance calculations, and route planning.
- **Radios for navigation and communication:** Provide access to navigational aids and air traffic control.

Setting Up Instruments and Avionics

- **Stepping into the Cockpit:** Choose your preferred aircraft first, and then load it into the cockpit. To have total control over the avionics panels, make sure you are seated in the pilot's seat.
- **Turn the aircraft on:** After turning on the aircraft, the avionics setup must be completed:
    - **Battery:** Select the 'ON' setting on the battery switch.
    - **Avionics Master Switch:** This switch is turned on. The avionics systems will be powered by this switch.
- **Configuring the Multi-Function Display (MFD) and Primary Flight Display (PFD):** The aircraft's avionics panel or a touchscreen interface in the cockpit is often used to adjust PFD and MFD settings.
    - **Brightness and Contrast:** Depending on the existing lighting conditions, adjust the brightness and contrast to get a nice vision.
    - **Display Layout:** Set up the layout to display information that may be required, such as engine parameters on the PFD and navigation maps on the MFD.
- **Flight Management System (FMS) configuration:** An important part of flight planning and navigation is the FMS:
    - **Route Planning:** Enter the airways, waypoints, and departure and arrival airports into the FMS.
    - **Performance Settings:** To maximize flying settings, enter the aircraft's weight, fuel load, and other performance information.

> **Autopilot Integration:** For automated flight control, make sure the FMS and autopilot are connected.
+ **Set up radios for navigation and communication:** An effective radio configuration is essential for both navigation and communication:
  > **Communication Radios:** To communicate with Air Traffic Control (ATC), choose active and standby frequencies.
  > **Navigation Radios:** Adjust the VHF Omnidirectional Range (VOR), Instrument Landing System (ILS), and other navigational assistance frequencies in accordance with your flight plan.

Making Use of External Add-ons and Tools

Think of including extra tools and add-ons for improved usefulness and realism:
+ **Navigraph:** Offers current navigation data and charts to guarantee precise flight planning.
+ The SimBrief tool facilitates the creation of comprehensive flight plans that can be input into the FMS.
+ **RealSimGear G1000 Suite:** To provide a completely haptic experience, hardware for the G1000 avionics suite is included.

Solving Typical Problems

The following are some issues that might arise while setting avionics:
+ **Problems with Display:** Verify that the aircraft's electrical systems are set correctly and that the avionics master switch is switched on in the event that the displays are blank or not working.
+ **Issues with Radio Communication:** Make sure the radios are switched on and the appropriate frequencies are chosen.
+ **FMS Errors:** Verify the accuracy of the input data and make sure the FMS and autopilot system are linked correctly.

Flight Management System (FMS) programming

Many flight planning and navigational activities are automated by the FMS, which increases efficiency and realism. An overview of programming the FMS is given in this section, along with particulars about the Airbus A320, Boeing 737, and Cessna Citation CJ4 aircraft.

Overview of FMS Programming in General

Pilots may add and manage flight plans, arrivals, departures, and other important data using the MSFS 2024 FMS. **The following are the primary stages involved in programming the FMS:**

- **FMS Initialization:** After turning on the aircraft, access to the FMS interface is granted.
- Adding flight plan information, such as airports of origin and destination, waypoints, airways, and protocols.
- **Performance Data Configuration:** Set weights, takeoff and landing speeds, and other performance metrics.
- **Evaluate and Carry Out the Plan:** Verify the information entered and activate the flight plan.

The FMS programming of the Airbus A320

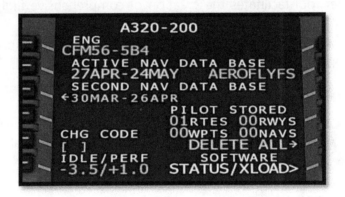

The Multi-Function handle and Display Unit is often used to handle the Airbus A320's Flight Management and Guidance System, or FMS.

Setting up

- Turn on the airplane and choose the MCDU.
- The initialization page may be accessed by clicking the INIT button.
- Enter the airports of origin and destination using the scratchpad and line select keys.

Entry of the Flight Plan

- To access the flight plan page, use the F-PLN button.
- Type the procedures, airways, and waypoints onto the scratchpad and then paste them into the corresponding areas.

Performance Information

- To access the performance page, use the PERF button.
- Enter weights, takeoff and landing speeds, and more performance metrics.

Evaluation and Implementation

- Examine the information submitted on MCDU.
- To start the flight plan, press the EXEC button.

Programming for the Boeing 737 FMS

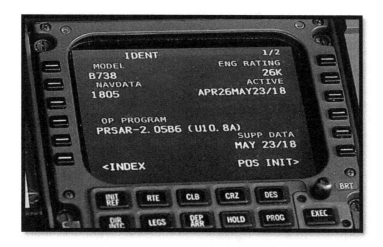

The Boeing 737's FMS uses the Multi-Function Control Display Unit, or MCDU, to do this.

Setting up

- Switch the aircraft on and turn on the MCDU.
- To see an initializing page, click the INIT button.
- Enter the airports of origin and destination.

Entry of the Flight Plan

- To see the flight plan page, press the FPLN button.
- Add procedures, airways, and waypoints.

Performance Information

- To see a performance page, click the PERF button.
- Enter weights, takeoff and landing speeds, and more performance metrics.

Evaluation and Implementation

 + Examine the data that was entered.
 + To activate the flight plan, press the EXEC button.

Citation CJ4 FMS Programming Cessna

The Cessna Citation CJ4's FMS is activated via the Control Display Unit (CDU) and Multi-Function Display (MFD).

Setting up

 + Open the CDU after turning on the aircraft.
 + To access the FMS pages, use the FMS button.

Entry of the Flight Plan

 + Enter the airports of origin and destination.
 + The addition of procedures, airways, and waypoints.

Performance Information

 + Enter weights, takeoff and landing speeds, and more performance metrics.

Evaluation and Implementation

 + Examine the data that was added.
 + Make the flight plan active.

Air Traffic Control (ATC) communication

Understanding MSFS 2024's ATC

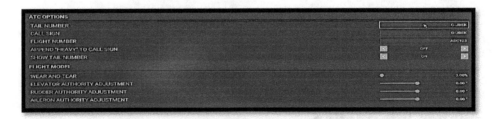

The integrated ATC system in MSFS 2024 closely mimics actual aviation traffic. This system manages the many stages of flight, including arrival, en route navigation, and departure. To properly communicate, the pilot has to be conversant with the ATC interface and its features.

How to Use the ATC Interface

The ATC window in MSFS 2024 may be accessed via the in-game menu or by setting up a keybinding that opens this window exclusively. For simple toggling, some have suggested making "Open Communications Panel" a key.

ATC Pre-Flight Protocols

- **Flight Planning:** Use the in-game flight planning tools to choose your departure and destination airports, waypoints, and altitudes before beginning a trip. Interactions with ATC throughout the flight are made easier with a well-prepared flight plan.
- **Flight Plan Filing:** The flight planning interface in MSFS 2024 allows you to submit a flight plan straight from inside. This helps ATC manage aviation traffic in a cooperative manner by informing them of your path.
- **Pre-Departure Communication:** Request permission to use a cab by calling ground control before to departure. Before you state your intentions, open the ATC window and choose the proper frequency.

ATC Communication in Flight

- **Departure:** As directed by ground control, change to the departure control frequency after takeoff. To get altitude allocations and navigation directions, stay in touch.
- **En Route:** You can be transferred to several ATC sectors while traveling. Keep an eye out for frequency changes in the ATC window and act quickly when directed.
- **Approach and Landing:** Call approach control for landing and sequencing instructions as you get closer to your destination. For a safe approach, adhere to the altitude allocations and vectors.

Advice for Successful ATC Interaction

- **Conciseness and Clarity:** Talk to ATC in a clear and succinct manner. Don't offer them more information than they need; just provide what is absolutely necessary.
- **Standard Phraseology:** To make sure everyone understands, get acquainted with the standard ATC phraseology. This relates to how to properly use terms for requests, acknowledgments, and directions.
- **Stay Up to Date:** Since the simulation environment will be changing over time, keep an eye out for any upgrades or modifications to ATC operations in MSFS 2024.

CHAPTER SEVEN
ABOUT TAKING-OFF AND TAXIING

Turning on the Engine

In MSFS 2024, starting the engine is a simple procedure that differs depending on the aircraft. Understanding the specific starting procedure is essential for a successful flight, regardless of whether you're piloting a complicated multi-engine jet like the Airbus A320neo or a little single-engine propeller aircraft like the Cessna 172 Skyhawk.

General Procedures for MSFS 2024 Engine Starting

- **Turn on the airplane:** Turn on the avionics and batteries of the airplane. Press the on button on the battery switch. Usually, this is located on the side console or overhead panel.
- **Set Throttle and Mixture Controls:** When the mixture is at rich, piston-engine aircraft should be put on idle. The throttle of a jet aircraft should be at the idle position.
- **Turn on the starter by pressing the switch or button**: Start keeping an eye on the engine instruments right away to see whether the engine is starting properly.
- **Set Engine:** Adjust the throttle and mixture for piston engines to the proper settings after the engine has started. To make sure the jet engines settle on their own, the N1 and N2 Revolutions per Minute (RPMs) should be monitored.

Procedures for Aircraft-Specific Startup

The Cessna 172 Skyhawk

- Set the throttle to idle and the mixture to rich.
- After turning on the starter, keep an eye on the RPM gauge.
- After starting the engine, adjust the mixture's lean and set the throttle to 1,000 RPM.

The Airbus A320neo

- The airplane needs to be dark and chilly.
- Activate the airplane by turning on the external power source and batteries.
- 'IGN/START' should be selected as the engine mode. Press the engine start push button's PWR button.

- Keep an eye on the engine's characteristics and adjust them as needed.

Atlas Airbus A400M

- Turn on the external power source and batteries.
- To provide electrical power, turn on the APU (Auxiliary Power Unit).
- Sequentially start the engines while keeping an eye on their individual settings.

Extra Advice

- **Use Checklists:** It is recommended to follow the particular starting instructions found in the checklist for the aircraft being flown.
- **Monitor Engine Settings:** During starting, pay attention to the temperature, oil pressure, and RPM gauges.
- **Practice Often:** To improve your skills, get familiar with various aircraft starts.

Reaching the Runway by Taxi

Learn how the airport is laid out before you start a taxi ride. Through the in-game navigation system, players may obtain comprehensive airport maps in MSFS 2024. These maps help you plan your path from the parking place to the active runway by showing you the runways, taxiways, and parking areas.

Making Use of the Taxi Ribbon

In MSFS 2024, there is a feature called "Taxi Ribbon" that will draw a route on the ground where you must walk in order to taxi.

To activate the Taxi Ribbon:
- Press the Esc key to bring up the menu.
- Press the "Assistance Options." button.
- Go to "Navigation," and turn "Taxi Ribbon" "On."

In order to assist you avoid getting lost on the incorrect taxi route, this activates the ribbon for you to follow.

Air Traffic Control (ATC) communication

The secret is to communicate with ATC effectively. Get authorization to taxi after pushback by contacting ground control. Instructions about the runway to be used and any particular taxi routes to be taken will be provided by the ATC. Read back instructions at all times, and report your position if needed.

Procedures for Taxation

- **Pushback and Engine Start:** To begin, you must ask for pushback from where you are parked. Start your engines as soon as it's clear.
- **Taxiing:** To begin moving the aircraft, the parking brake is removed and a little throttle is applied. Align the aircraft with the taxiway's centerline by using the rudder to steer.
- **Speed Control:** Depending on the kind of aircraft and the size of the airport, safe taxi speeds typically range from 10 to 20 knots.
- **Monitoring Instruments:** Make sure all systems are working within their typical ranges by periodically looking inside at the engine parameters and other instruments.
- **Following Directions:** As soon as possible, and with the utmost accuracy, follow ATC's directions. Ask for explanation if you are given instructions on anything you do not understand.

Managing Airports without Control

It is your responsibility to announce your location and intentions at uncontrolled airports. Make sure there is no other traffic in the vicinity before announcing your intentions on the proper frequency before approaching a runway to leave. Keep an eye out for other planes at all times.

Executing Takeoff Protocols

Both inexperienced and seasoned virtual pilots must become proficient in these processes.

- **Preparations Prior to Takeoff:** Make sure the following actions are taken before starting a takeoff in MSFS 2024:
  - ➤ Examine your flight plan, taking note of the runway allocations, departure airport, and Standard Instrument Departure (SID) protocols. Understanding the anticipated path and any special instructions requires this planning.
  - ➤ **Aircraft Configuration:** As directed by the manufacturer, set up the aircraft's systems for flight. This would include adjusting the beginning altitude, navigation radios, and autopilot. A seamless transition from takeoff to cruising is ensured by proper arrangement.
  - ➤ **Weather Assessment:** Examine the present weather, taking note of visibility, wind speed and direction, and any noteworthy weather occurrences. Runway selection and takeoff performance calculations are influenced by this information.
- **Reaching the Runway by Taxi:** After preparing for the trip, take a taxi to the designated runway:
  - ➤ **Taxi Clearance:** The ground control should give you the all-clear to board the taxi. If there are any special instructions, make sure you are following the correct runway.
  - ➤ **Taxi Procedures:** Take the designated taxi route while in a cab. Observe speed restrictions and stay short of runways as directed. To prevent accidents and guarantee safe ground movement, be mindful of your surroundings.
  - ➤ **Final Checks:** Verify everything one more time before stepping onto the runway, including the takeoff configuration, engine performance, and flaps.
- **Getting in line and taking off:** Take off from the runway's threshold by:
  - ➤ **Line-Up:** The aircraft is in the proper take-off position, the nose wheel is straight, and it is parallel to the runway centerline.
  - ➤ **Takeoff Clearance:** Get the tower's takeoff clearance, which is only an indication that the runway is clear and you may go forward.
  - ➤ **Throttle Advance:** To take off power, smoothly advance the throttle while keeping an eye on the engine's instruments to make sure they stay within safe operating bounds.
  - ➤ **Brakes remove:** To begin the takeoff roll, smoothly remove the brakes while using the rudder pedals to retain direction control.

- > **Rotation:** Pull back on the yoke or control column to raise the nose wheel off the runway and point the nose upward to begin the climb as the aircraft accelerates and reaches the proper speed (after V1 speed is reached).
- > **Ascent-Out:** As you increase speed and altitude, gradually retract the flaps while maintaining a steady ascent rate. For the appropriate climb performance, adjust the engines' power levels as necessary.
- **Procedures After Takeoff:** Following takeoff, execute the following actions:
  - > **Flap Retraction:** In accordance with the operation handbook, gradually retract the flaps. Preserve the airspeed so that it doesn't go beyond the designated limit.
  - > **Landing Gear:** To reduce drag and improve climb efficiency, retract the landing gear at a safe height.
  - > **Autopilot Engagement:** If autopilot is fitted and desired, activate it during the ascent and navigation, adjusting the settings for the subsequent flying phase.
  - > **ATS Communication:** Call position reports, contact the proper departure frequency under ATC, and get further instructions.
- **Typical Problems and Advice:**
  - > **Speed Control:** During takeoff and climb-out, careful attention must be paid to airspeed. Exceeding the allowed speed limit may possibly result in loss of control or structural damage. To prevent overspeeding, use the climb and cruise power levels that are shown on the engine instrument.
  - > **Workload Management:** In high-performance aircraft, the early ascent period might be difficult. Use the maxim "Aviate, Navigate, Communicate" to help you prioritize your tasks:
    - ✓ **Aviate:** The plane should be controlled and ascending as intended.
    - ✓ **Navigate:** As necessary, set course and activate navigation systems.
    - ✓ **Communicate:** Get in touch with ATC and provide the required position reports.
  - > **Autopilot Usage:** Using the autopilot might lessen effort, but make sure it is set up correctly first. To operate the autopilot systems efficiently, get familiar with them.
  - > **Situational Awareness:** Keep an eye on tools and outside circumstances at all times to foresee and react quickly to changes.
- **Practice and Instruction:** To become proficient in takeoff techniques, regular practice is necessary:

- ➤ **Flight Training:** Practice takeoff techniques in a variety of aircraft and situations by using MSFS 2024's training modules.
- ➤ **Scenario Practice:** Construct unique scenarios under a range of takeoff circumstances, including weather, runway length, and changes in aircraft weight.
- ➤ **Evaluate and Learn:** After each flight, evaluate your performance, identify areas for development, and ask instructors or the MSFS community for guidance.

Handling Climb-Out

A seamless transition from takeoff to cruising altitude in MSFS 2024 depends heavily on the management of the climb-out phase. **For safety and efficiency, it entails modifying the aircraft's settings for the phase, monitoring performance, and according to established protocols.**

- ✦ **Procedures After Takeoff:** Following liftoff, the following has to be taken into account:
  - ➤ **Retraction of Landing Gear and Flaps:** After reaching a safe altitude, retract the landing gear and then lower the flaps to the takeoff position.
  - ➤ **Set Thrust to Climb Power Settings:** For jet aircraft, this should be lowered to climb power of around 85–90% N1 for maximum fuel efficiency and long life.
  - ➤ **Climb pace Setting:** It's important to maintain a climb pace that strikes a balance between fuel efficiency and performance. It is usually provided by the aircraft's FMS; if not, it is manually adjusted according to the weight and type of aircraft.
- ✦ **Controlling the Weight and Balance of the Aircraft:** An even weight distribution is essential for a steady climb:
  - ➤ **Center of Gravity (CG):** The CG must fall inside the aircraft's specified bounds. An aircraft with poor balance will either rise too high or be unable to stay in the air. Set the CG in MSFS 2024 by adjusting the aircraft selection menu's weight and balance.
  - ➤ **Gasoline and cargo Distribution:** To keep everything balanced, distribute the gasoline and cargo. For example, CG may be impacted by placing cargo at the back of the aircraft, requiring changes to the trim settings or fuel distribution.
- ✦ **Cut Out Settings:** Appropriate trim settings improve climb stability and lower control pressures:

- ➢ **Elevator Trim:** Without continuous control input, adjust the elevator trim to maintain the intended ascent attitude. This is particularly true for aircraft that may need a lot of adjustment during climb-out, such as the Boeing 787.
- ➢ **Trim Monitoring:** Throughout the ascent, periodically check and correct the trim since fuel use and aircraft weight reduction may alter the climb's characteristics.
- ✦ **Systems for flight management and autopilot:** Using the FMS and autopilot may help you ascend more efficiently:
  - ➢ **Turn on Autopilot:** To control climb settings, turn on the autopilot as soon as you take off. Decide on the necessary height, vertical speed, or angle of the flight route.
  - ➢ **Flight Plan Integration:** To ensure a smooth ascent, make sure the flight plan and its waypoints with altitude limits are correctly input into the FMS.
  - ➢ **Track Performance:** In order to maintain climb performance characteristics within their optimal range, such as vertical speed, airspeed, and engine settings, it is important to continually track them throughout a climb.
- ✦ **Fuel management and engine performance:** During a climb, efficient engine operation is essential:
  - ➢ **Engine parameters:** To ensure peak climbing performance, modify the engine parameters. Leaning the mixture, for instance, may enhance climb performance in the Cessna 172, particularly at higher altitudes.
  - ➢ **Fuel Consumption:** Keep an eye on fuel consumption rates to make sure there is enough for the duration of the flight, and modify engine settings and climb rates as needed to maximize fuel efficiency.
- ✦ **Following the Directions of Air Traffic Control (ATC):** Effective communication using ATC is accomplished by:
  - ➢ **Altitude Assignments:** Adhere to the established heights that ATC has allocated and promptly report any variations.
  - ➢ **Speed Limitations:** Typically, ATC will either include speed restrictions in the flight plan or impose them during climb-out.
  - ➢ **Position Reports:** In most cases, when radar coverage is unavailable, a position report must be sent.
- ✦ **Tracking the Weather:** A large portion of the climb performance is determined by the weather:
  - ➢ **Wind and Turbulence:** Pay attention to wind and turbulence since they may impact aircraft stability or climb rates.
  - ➢ **Temperature and Pressure:** Recognize how engine performance and climb rates are affected by temperature and air pressure.

- ➢ **Weather Updates:** To prevent unfavorable situations, periodically review weather updates and modify the climb profile as needed.
- ✦ **Practice and Instruction:** Climb-out competence may be developed with regular practice:
  - ➢ **Simulated Flights:** To build confidence and muscle memory, concentrate on the climb-out process during simulated flights.
  - ➢ **Scenario Training:** To be ready for any unforeseen circumstances during climb-out, practice several scenarios like as engine failure or bad weather.
  - ➢ **Review Procedures:** To ensure the utmost professionalism, periodically review climb-out protocols and performance charts unique to each aircraft.

Activating Autopilot Mechanisms

The MSFS 2024 autopilot systems are designed to replicate the actions of their real-world equivalents, providing the user with a very thorough and realistic flying experience. Altitude, speed, direction, and navigation are all handled by these systems, freeing up the pilot to focus on other crucial aspects of flight control.

Using Autopilot to Help with Taxing

Despite the fact that traditional autopilot systems are not used during taxiing, MSFS 2024 adds capabilities that assist pilots in this phase:
- ✦ **Auto-Tuning of Frequencies:** During aircraft taxiing, the simulator automatically adjusts radio frequencies to facilitate prompt contact with ATC. This function enhances situational awareness and reduces workload.
- ✦ **Pre-programmed Routes:** Pilots may enter departure routes into the simulator, and the aircraft will automatically taxi along a predetermined path. In large, complex airports with several taxiways, this is quite helpful.

Turning on Autopilot While Flying

The steps listed below must be followed in order to activate the autopilot system for takeoff on MSFS 2024:
- ✦ **Flight Plan Input:** Pilots may use the simulator's Flight Management System (FMS) to build up their flight plan before to takeoff. It is possible to enter desired heights, airways, and waypoints.
- ✦ **Autopilot Settings:** Pilots may choose their preferred autopilot settings after entering their flight plan. This involves deciding on the preferred direction, speed, and altitude.

- **Autopilot Engagement:** The pilot may control the climb, navigation, and cruise stages of the flight by activating the autopilot system as soon as the aircraft lifts off. While adhering to a flight plan, this might make flying simpler for the pilot.

Realistic Aspects

Although MSFS 2024's autopilot system is quite reliable, there are a few things a pilot should be aware of:

- **Manual Override:** Pilots have the option to manually take control of the autopilot at any time, which is required in certain unanticipated situations or if a deviation from the flight plan is required.
- **System Limitations:** Each aircraft has both strengths and weaknesses. For example, several aircraft types have specific protocols for activating autopilot during taking off.
- **Training and Familiarization:** In MSFS 2024, specific autopilot systems in various aircraft types should be thoroughly examined. Each could have unique characteristics and ways of working.

CHAPTER EIGHT

NAVIGATING THE IN-FLIGHT

Comprehending Flight Levels and Airspace

Airspace is divided into many categories, each with its own rules and procedures for use. These classes are accurately designed to reflect actual aviation regulations in MSFS 2024.

- Class A airspace is defined as the area between 18,000 and 60,000 feet above mean sea level (MSL). All aircraft must fly inside this area, which is designated for Instrument Flight Rules.
- Class B Airspace: Usually forming around the busiest airports, this area extends from the surface to 10,000 feet above sea level and is intended to keep high-density traffic apart. Entry into this area needs authorization from air traffic management.
- Airspace classified as Class C extends up to 4,000 feet above the airport's elevation. Before entering, pilots should establish a two-way radio connection with the commanding facility.
- Class D Airspace: This area reaches 2,500 feet above the airport's elevation from the ground. Before each pilot enters, two-way radio connection must be established with the controlling facility.
- Controlled airspace not labeled A, B, C, or D is included in class E airspace. The typical range is 1,200 feet above sea level to 18,000 feet above sea level.
- The uncontrolled area that is beyond the lines of regulated airspace is known as class G airspace. It stretches up to 1,200 feet above sea level and, in some places, up to 14,500 feet above mean sea level.

In order to allow its users to experience the intricacies of airspace management and navigation, MSFS 2024 has accurately recreated these classifications of airspace.

Altimeter settings and flight levels

In order to keep other aircraft securely apart, these heights are flying levels that were defined to be hundreds of feet. **In MSFS 2024, accurate navigation greatly depends on an altimeter that is configured correctly.**

- **Transition Altitude:** The altitude at which a pilot switches from local altimeter settings to the standard setting of 29.92 inHg is known as the transition altitude. This height is typically 18,000 feet above sea level in the United States. The altimeter should be adjusted to the regular setting after reaching this height.

- **Flight Levels (FL):** Flight levels are altitudes above the transition altitude. FL300, for example, indicates 30,000 feet MSL. Flight levels are used for separation and are measured in hundreds of feet.
- **Standard Altimeter Setting:** Pilots adjust their altimeters to the standard pressure setting of 29.92 inHg above the changeover altitude. Safe separation is made possible by this standardization, which guarantees that all aircraft are referring to the same pressure level.

These concepts have been sufficiently represented in MSFS 2024 to allow users to practice appropriate altimeter settings and comprehend how they affect navigation.

Useful Implementation in MSFS 2024

For efficient navigation inside MSFS 2024, the pilots might perform the following:
- **Filing Flight Plan Routes with Airspace Classes:** To appropriately plan the entrance and exit requirements of each class of airspace, consult the flight-planned route of airspace classes to be encountered prior to the flight.
- **Properly Set Altimeters:** Set the altimeter to the standard setting above the transition altitude and the local setting below it. Once again, this gives precise altitude data for reporting and mimics how it is carried out in a real-world situation.
- **Contact with ATC:** If you need to, such when you're entering a regulated area, get in touch with ATC. The simulation's realism is further increased by MSFS 2024's patterned ATC, which is comparable to the actual system.
- **Track Flight Levels:** Be aware of the flight levels that are given and suitable for the flight direction. In the United States, for example, planes heading east are often allocated odd flight levels (like FL310) while those heading west are assigned even flight levels (like FL320). When two airplanes are flying in different directions, the system helps keep them apart.

Making Use of Navigation Aids (GPS, NDB, VOR)

With its comprehensive in-flight navigation, MSFS 2024 offers great practice with a variety of navigational aids, including GPS (Global Positioning System), NDB (Non-Directional Beacon), and VOR (VHF Omnidirectional Range). For virtual pilots, mastering all three is essential, but those with more realistic aviation goals will find it as fascinating and helpful.

VHF Omnidirectional Range, or VOR

A ground-based radio navigation system called VOR gives airplanes azimuth information so the pilot can figure out where they are and what direction to steer. Pilots may receive signals by tuning onto precise frequencies in MSFS 2024, which faithfully models VORs.

Making use of VOR

- **Selecting the VOR Frequency:** Turn on the aircraft's navigation radio panel and enter the preferred VOR frequency. The in-game radio tuning interface or the aircraft's avionics may be used for this.
- **Setting the Course:** On the navigation screen of your aircraft, choose the appropriate course heading. Usually, Horizontal Situation Indicator or Course Deviation Indicator controls are used for this.
- **Tracking the VOR Signal and Interception:** Fly in the direction of the VOR station until you catch the required radial. The CDI or HSI will alert you to lateral deviation so you can remain on track once you're on it.

Non-Directional Beacon, or NDB

NDBs are radio transmitters that are situated on the ground and broadcast in all directions. With an Automatic Direction Finder (ADF) installed, the aircraft can precisely calculate its bearing based on the NDB's location. Many of these NDBs are still available in MSFS 2024 as a useful tool for navigation practice, even if they are used less often now because of advancements in navigation technology.

Making use of the NDB

- **Tuning the ADF:** Using the aircraft's avionics or the radio tune interface included in the game, the ADF is adjusted to the desired NDB's necessary frequency.
- **Find the NDB:** The ADF needle begins to show a bearing to it when it is tuned. According to navigational regulations, this necessitates changing the aircraft directions such that flying is either into or away from it.

- **Follow the NDB:** Continue following the intended bearing to the NDB, making necessary course adjustments.

Things to Think About

Since many NDBs have already been deactivated in favor of GPS navigation, there isn't much in the field of NDBs anymore. A mode on MSFS 2024, however, allows for the restoration of more than 4,500 NDBs in addition to VORs and DMEs, allowing for conventional radio navigation on older aircraft.

The GPS (Global Positioning System)

GPS is a satellite-based navigation system that offers precise and dependable position and timing data, making it revolutionary for navigation. This GPS integration in MSFS 2024 is dependent on the avionics suite of the aircraft.

Making use of GPS

- Depending on the aircraft, the GPS unit may be accessible via a multifunction display or incorporated into the avionics panel.
- **Route Programming:** Enter desired waypoints, airways, or destinations into the GPS flight plan using the avionics controls on the aircraft or the in-game GPS interface.
- **Turning on the Flight Plan:** To fly the preprogrammed path, turn on the autopilot's navigation mode. To keep on track, the aircraft automatically adjusts its direction.

Including Navigational Aids

Pilots may improve situational awareness and navigation accuracy in MSFS 2024 by integrating several navigation aids. These include the use of GPS for accurate approach procedures and VORs for en route navigation.

Useful Advice

- **Cross-Referencing Navigation Aids:** In regions with spotty GPS coverage, use VORs and NDBs to confirm location while in flight.
- **Switching Between Navigation Aids:** Switch to GPS navigation for ongoing guidance when the time is right, before an area with restricted VOR or NDB coverage is reached.

- **Monitoring Navigation Systems:** To ensure good functioning and accurate information display, all navigation systems should undergo routine inspections.

Keeping an eye on fuel use

A number of variables, including aircraft type, flight altitude, speed, and engine setting, affect fuel consumption in MSFS 2024. Every aircraft model uses fuel at a different rate, which varies based on a number of operational factors.

Keeping an eye on fuel usage

Pilots in MSFS 2024 may keep an eye on fuel use using a variety of instruments and methods:
- **Instruments in the Cockpit:** The majority of the aircraft in MSFS 2024 include instruments for fuel flow indication, which will display the rates of fuel use in real time. Pilots will therefore be able to make necessary modifications during flight as they would get immediate input about fuel usage.
- **Flight Planning Tools:** One example of a flight planning tool is SimBrief, which estimates the amount of fuel needed before a flight starts based on the intended route, aircraft type, and weather prediction. This aids in calculating additional requirements throughout the flight and setting accurate fuel loads.
- **In-Flight Monitoring:** Throughout the flight, it is necessary to routinely monitor the amount and rate of fuel use. This will make it easier to identify any differences between the anticipated and actual fuel usage, allowing for prompt action if needed.

Advice for Increasing Fuel Efficiency

Fuel economy improves the entire flying experience and increases realism. Here are some pointers for getting the most fuel efficiency:
- **Flight Path Optimization:** Utilize flight planning software to determine the most cost-effective path while accounting for airspace constraints and wind patterns.
- Adjusting the throttle settings and keeping the engines running within the advised ranges both significantly reduce fuel usage.
- **Weight/Balance Monitoring:** For maximum efficiency, the aircraft is typically loaded within the weight and balance parameters.
- **Use autopilot sparingly:** Although it may assist in maintaining the aircraft's path and altitude, human adjustments are necessary for the best fuel efficiency, which is particularly feasible during the climb and descent stages.

Resolving Problems with Fuel Consumption

Pilots operating in MSFS 2024 may sometimes encounter a variety of fuel-related issues, including as sudden fuel depletion or differences between anticipated and actual fuel use. **In these situations, do the following:**

- **Verify Aircraft Settings:** If any of the aircraft's systems are not configured properly, fuel consumption may increase.
- **Examine the Flight Plan:** Verify the correctness of the flight plan to make sure the parameters used to calculate fuel are realistic.
- Engage in MSFS community forums and resources by consulting the community resources. Other pilots may sometimes provide a tip on how to resolve these problems. The fuel consumption problem with some aircraft types, such the DHC-2, was discovered by a simple search in a Reddit topic. Some advice on fuel conservation was exchanged.
- Modify Simulation Settings: Users who use time compression or other simulation modifications should be aware that this further modifies the fuel consumption rate. Several findings indicate that fuel consumption does not rise proportionally with an increase in simulation speed, which accounts for the whole variation in fuel consumption.

Real-World Example: Boosting Career Mode

Sometimes there isn't enough fuel on board for the desired flight for pilots operating in MSFS 2024 Career Mode. By assigning a button or key to the "Add Fuel" action, pilots may do this while in flight.

Once activated throughout the flight, it will gradually provide gasoline, allowing the pilots to finish their missions with little loss of realism. People's experiences and remedies for the several problems caused by a shortage of gasoline have been addressed on the MSFS forums.

Adapting to the Weather

MSFS 2024 properly simulates atmospheric conditions with the use of sophisticated weather simulation. The game's installation size is reduced to around 30GB thanks to its cloud-based design and comprehensive weather streaming on demand. This will guarantee that the weather is as accurate and relevant to the flight route and location as possible.

Getting to and Modifying Weather Preferences

Using the World Map Planner, the pilot may modify the flight weather before to takeoff by selecting the 'Weather and Time' option, live weather, one of the several pre-set weather scenarios, or a custom configuration. It offers a great deal of flexibility in producing a realistic flying environment or in completing special weather-specific flying tasks. In-flight modifications are also possible. To modify weather factors such as wind direction, velocity, overcast, and precipitation, launch the in-game menu and click on the weather icon. In training scenarios or while flying into unforeseen weather, this is helpful.

Important Weather Events and How They Affect Flight

Numerous weather events, each of which interacts differently with flight dynamics, are properly modeled by MSFS 2024:

- **Clouds and Visibility:** Flight planning and visibility are impacted by the realistic forms and densities shown by advanced cloud visuals. Pilots must adapt their navigational tactics to low visibility situations, such as fog or gloomy weather.
- **Wind:** The simulator simulates wind patterns that affect aircraft control, particularly during takeoff and landing, such as turbulence and crosswinds. Therefore, in order to maintain control and guarantee safety, pilots need anticipate and account for wind impacts.
- **Weather and Precipitation:** Rain and snow have an impact on lift and engine efficiency, among other aspects of aircraft performance. Pilots must modify their speed, altitude, and approach angles to account for realistic precipitation simulation in MSFS 2024.

- **Temperature and Humidity:** Variations in these two variables may alter air density, which can impact lift and engine performance. Pilots should consider these considerations while calculating takeoff distances and fuel needs.

Useful Tips for Weather Adaptation

- **Pre-Flight Planning:** Utilize MSFS 2024 weather predictions to ascertain the anticipated flight path. This is crucial for altitude selection, fuel calculations, and route planning.
- During the flight, keep an eye out for weather updates. Pilots will be able to make well-informed judgments on route and altitude changes because to MSFS 2024's ability to offer real-time weather updates.
- **Aircraft Performance Modifications:** Be ready to modify aircraft settings in response to weather conditions. For example, aircraft speed must be maintained by increasing engine power in the presence of severe headwinds, while flying stability in turbulent circumstances necessitates adjusting autopilot settings.
- **Emergency Preparedness:** In the event of inclement weather, such as thunderstorms or ice, be ready for emergency protocols. Engine icing and electrical problems are realistic simulations in MSFS 2024 that need prompt and accurate reactions.

Education and the Development of Skills

For pilot training, MSFS 2024's realistic weather simulation is an excellent resource. A pilot will be able to manage challenging circumstances and make better judgments if they practice in a variety of weather conditions. Every flight is unique due to the simulator's dynamic weather, which guarantees an ongoing learning process.

Interaction with ATC En Route

The foundation of aviation efficiency and safety is good communication with Air Traffic Control (ATC). Interacting with ATC while flying in Microsoft Flight Simulator 2024 (MSFS 2024) improves realism and makes flying more enjoyable. Pilots will be able to communicate with virtual controllers throughout their flight thanks to MSFS 2024's integrated ATC system. **Clearances, route modifications, and traffic warnings are all managed by the system. Typically, the procedure entails:**

- **Primary Contact:** Making contact with the departing ATC as soon as you take off.
- Maintaining constant communication with ATC centers while flying is known as "en route communication."

- **Approach and Landing:** arranging landing clearances in coordination with approach controllers.

Configuring ATC Communication

To begin contacting with the ATC about MSFS 2024:
- **Activate the ATC Panel:** To open the ATC window, press the default keybinding, which is often Scroll Lock. Additionally, to make opening the panel more comfortable, give the "Open Communications Panel" function a unique key or button.
- **Choose the Correct Frequency:** Select the frequency of the particular ATC you want to contact on the game's radio panel. Verify that you are set to the appropriate frequency for your location and flight phase.
- **Start Communication:** To access the communication options, click on the ATC window. To submit your message to ATC, choose the relevant option.

En Route Communication

It's critical to be in constant contact with ATC throughout the en route period. This comprises:
- **Position Reports:** Inform ATC of your objectives, position, and altitude.
- **Altitude modifications:** Asking for and getting approval for altitude modifications.
- **Route Deviations:** Notifying ATC of any deviations from the intended path.
- Information about other aircraft activity in the area is provided by traffic advisories.

Utilizing ATC Add-Ons from Third Parties

Incorporate third-party add-ons for a more sophisticated and realistic ATC:
- **Pilot2ATC:** Supports both IFR and VFR flights and provides speech recognition.
- **ProATC/SR:** Offers background ATC communications and voice recognition.
- **BeyondATC:** AI technology is used to facilitate ATC communication.
- **SayIntentions.AI:** An AI-driven ATC system that enables natural-sounding spoken interaction between users.

Your interactions with ATC may become much more sophisticated and realistic with the help of these technologies.

Tips for ATC Communication

- **Standard Phraseology:** Using accepted aviation communication practices guarantees lucidity and minimizes miscommunications.

- **Be Brief:** For effective communication, make sure your communications are succinct, understandable, and direct.
- **Listen Carefully:** To ensure that the message is understood, pay great attention to ATC and repeat back clearances.
- **Stay Current:** Check for updates or changes to ATC procedures from inside the simulator on a regular basis.

Typical Problems and Solutions

The following problems with ATC in MSFS 2024 have been noted by users:
- **Unresponsive ATC Window:** Restarting the simulator may fix an unresponsive ATC window.
- **Loss of ATC Sound:** Occasionally, during flight, ATC sound may be lost. In many cases, restarting the simulator will restore this.
- **ATC Losing Interest:** Following updates, some users have reported that ATC has become less communicative. This might be addressed as well, since the creators welcome user input.

CHAPTER NINE
METHODS AND LANDING

Organizing the Descent

One of the most important flight phases in MSFS 2024 is descent planning, which calls for extensive planning and skillful execution to manage the approach to a safe and effective landing. The TOC calculation, speed and altitude control, aircraft design, and adherence to standard operating procedures are some of the crucial phases that will be included in that process. **Pilots may improve their flying skills and make flawless landings by understanding these concepts.**

- **The Top of Descent (TOD) calculation:** The term "top of descent" refers to the starting point for your fall from your cruise altitude to the airport of destination. As a general guideline, begin the descent three nautical miles from the airport for every 1,000 feet of height that will be lost. For example, you may begin your descent around 90 nautical miles from the airport if you are flying at 30,000 feet and need to land at sea level. You may make adjustments based on weather conditions and air traffic control directions, and this computation will provide you with a controlled and progressive fall.

- **Controlling Speed and Altitude:** Maintaining the right fall speed and altitude is crucial. Reduce the power first so that the aircraft may begin to descend and avoid exceeding the safe airspeed. Then, based on the type and weight of the aircraft, adjust your fall rate to be between 1,000 and 1,500 feet per minute using the pitch of the aircraft. Check the VSI often to make sure the fall rate doesn't exceed a predetermined threshold.

- **Aircraft Setup:** The aircraft should be configured correctly to regulate speed and stability throughout your descent:
  - **Flaps:** Reduce speed while extending flaps in a predetermined way. This maintains the aircraft's lift and control. Consult operating manuals for instructions on how to deploy flaps depending on certain speeds and altitudes for every given aircraft model.
  - **Landing Gear:** Usually extended on the last approach, however the nature of the aircraft and the approach being flown greatly influence this.
  - **Autopilot and Autothrust:** Adjust heading and altitude with the autopilot. For speed control, use the autothrust. To monitor the approach method, make the necessary adjustments.

- **Observing SOPs:** Standard operating procedures, or SOPs, must be adhered to for a safe descent:

➢ **Briefing:** A landing briefing and appropriate approach are required. Along with the anticipated weather and any risks, the approach chart will be addressed.
➢ **Checklists:** Make sure that everything is completed during the descent phase by using pertinent checklists.
➢ **Communications:** Pay attention to ATC position reports and respond appropriately by receiving descents.
✦ **Utilizing the Features of MSFS 2024:** There are a number of aspects in MSFS 2024 that are useful for determining the optimum way to organize a descent:
➢ **Flight Planning Tools:** Create and edit flight plans, including descent profiles, using the in-game flight planning tools.
➢ **Navigation Aids:** To help with the descent and approach phases, use navigation aids including VORs, NDBs, and ILS systems.
➢ **Weather Integration:** Real-time weather data is included into MSFS 2024. This aids pilots in anticipating and becoming ready for any weather-related emergencies that may arise during the descent phase.
✦ **Practice and Ongoing Education:** It takes a lot of practice to really become proficient in descent planning. Try a range of situations. Trying out various weather conditions and aircraft types is a fantastic place to start. For proficient advice and the newest methods from seasoned pilots, check out sites like the MSFS 2024 forums and tutorials.

Getting Ready to Approach

Setting up the approach and landing successfully in MSFS 2024 requires careful preparation and precise execution.

It creates a smooth and seamless transition from cruising altitude to the ground, making it very realistic and immersive.

- **Planning before Approaching:** Choose your target airport and study its approach protocols first. For many airports throughout the globe, MSFS 2024 provides comprehensive charts and approach plates. Learn the various methods, such as the Visual Flight Rules (VFR), Instrument Landing System (ILS), or RNAV (Area Navigation) protocols.

- **Configuring the Flight Schedule:** Make a path from your starting point to your destination using the in-game flight planning tools. Make that the waypoints leading to the initial approach fix (IAF) of the approach method you have selected are included in your flight plan. During the approach phase, navigation is made smooth by this integration.

- **Examining the weather:** Get the most recent weather data for the airport where you are going. Real-time meteorological information, such as cloud cover, visibility, and wind direction and speed, is provided by MSFS 2024. It is essential to comprehend these factors in order to choose the best strategy and foresee any difficulties that may arise while landing.

- **Outlining the Approach Process:** To ascertain the order of waypoints, elevations, and any necessary turns, use the approach maps. Keep a careful eye on the missed approach, MDA, DA, and final approach courses. You can prepare for the particular that will be needed during the approach and landing thanks to this briefing.

- **Aircraft Setup:** Make sure your aircraft is configured correctly before beginning the approach.
  - **Autopilot Settings:** Select the lateral and vertical navigation modes to have the autopilot record the approach course.
  - **Navigation Radios:** It is necessary to adjust the navigation radios to the frequency of the ILS or other approach aids designated for that specific approach procedure.
  - **Flight Instruments:** To display the right height, the altimeter must be adjusted to the current local pressure setting.

- **Initiation of Descent:** Depending on the approach process and the rate of descent of your aircraft, begin your descent at the proper distance from the target. To avoid an excessive build-up of speed, maintain a regulated rate of descent. Utilize pitch to regulate the rate of fall and throttle to regulate airspeed.

- **Control of Speed and Configuration:** To enhance lift and drag and enable a slower approach speed, gradually extend the flaps as you descend. To prevent an aerodynamic stall, extend each flap setting at the suggested airspeeds or higher.

To maintain the proper approach speed, keep a careful eye on your speed and make any required adjustments to your throttle and pitch.

- **Complementing the Approach Course:** Align the aircraft with the approach course using the navigation systems. When using ILS approaches, the autopilot may be configured to monitor and record the glideslope for vertical guidance as well as the localizer for lateral guidance. Make that the aircraft is correctly following the GPS-guided flying route during RNAV approaches.
- **Last-Minute Approach and Landing:** Approach and Landing: As you approach the runway, keep an eye on your location in relation to the glide slope and runway centerline. To maintain the right approach profile, modify the speed and rate of descent. Unless you are in a situation where a landing is possible, you must immediately commence a missed approach or go around at the DA or MDA. Reduce your speed and lightly touch the runway to land when you approach the runway threshold.
- **Procedures Following Landing:** Retract the flaps after landing, use the brakes if necessary, and depart the runway via the first exit that opens. Complete the post-landing checklist by contacting ground control for taxi instructions, retracting the landing gear (if it is equipped), and turning off any lights that are not required.

Carrying Out Landing Procedures

- **Plan your Approach:** A decent plan is the first step in a good approach. To begin, familiarize yourself with the runway orientation, approach angles, and any obstructions by using the Instrument Landing System (ILS) or Visual Flight Rules (VFR) approach charts provided by the airport. These may be completed in MSFS 2024 using the in-game flight planning tool or by consulting outside resources.
- **Configuring the Aircraft:**
  - **Autopilot Configuration:** Set the aircraft's autopilot to the chosen approach mode if it has an automated approach. Make that the route is adjusted to match the runway heading and that both navigation radios are tuned to the right ILS frequency. After aligning with the ILS localizer, switch to the autopilot approach mode. Turn off the flight director and autopilot for complete control in the event of a manual landing.
  - **Speed and Flaps:** To preserve control and stability, the aircraft's speed should be set to the suggested approach speed. As one descends, the flaps should be extended in stages in accordance with the aircraft's instructions.
- **The Last Step**
  - **Glide Slope Capture:** Pay attention to the glide slope indication during landing. The airplane should be descending at a 3-degree angle, or on the

correct glide path. This angle of descent will be maintained if there is an autopilot system.

- ➢ **Visual References:** To verify alignment and descent rate, look for visual references such runway lights, runway markers, and PAPI lights. To aid in this process, MSFS 2024 has improved its visuals to provide realistic visual cues.

- ✦ **Deceleration in Midair**
  - ➢ **Speed Reduction:** For a steady approach, lower the speed to the suggested landing speed. To maintain control, steer clear of abrupt changes in height and speed.
  - ➢ **Landing Gear and Flaps:** As directed by the aircraft's operating handbook, extend the landing gear at the proper height and velocity. Flaps may be extended farther as needed to achieve the appropriate approach angle and velocity.

- ✦ **Landing**
  - ➢ **Flare:** To initiate the flare just before to landing, smoothly draw back on the stick or control yoke to lift the aircraft's nose. This slows down the rate of descent and enables the main wheels to make contact with the runway first.
  - ➢ **Touchdown Zone:** To give yourself ample time to stop, try landing in the first third of the runway. You may simulate realistic runway lengths and landing zones in MSFS 2024.

- ✦ **Braking on the Ground**
  - ➢ **Reverse Thrust:** This should start as soon as the aircraft touches down in order to help slow it down. The throttle controls in MSFS 2024 allow you to adjust the reverse thrust parameters.
  - ➢ **Braking:** To prevent skidding, smoothly use the wheel brakes. To decide when to safely quit the runway, keep an eye on the aircraft's speed and runway length.

- ✦ **Procedures Following Landing**
  - ➢ **Flaps and Gear:** After the aircraft has adequately slowed and cleared the runway, retract the flaps and landing gear.
  - ➢ **Taxiing:** To get to the assigned gate or parking location, according to the airport's taxiway regulations. ATC offers comprehensive taxi instructions in MSFS 2024 to help you navigate.

Taking a taxi to the gate

- ✦ **Procedures Following Landing:** Following a successful landing, regular protocols will be implemented for efficiency and safety:

- **Exit the Runway:** After landing and lowering your speed, use the in-game map or airport charts to determine which exit to take. Then, depart the runway at the designated taxiway.
- **Get in touch with Ground Control:** For taxi instructions, get in touch with Ground Control as soon as you are off the runway. This is done using the ATC menu in MSFS 2024. You may have to manually seek taxi instructions if Ground Control does not provide them to you.

- **Turn on the features that assist taxis:** The following features are available in MSFS 2024 to aid with ground navigation:
  - **Taxi Ribbon:** It shows a route to the gate or parking space where you have been allotted, using blue dots. To activate it:
    - ✓ Select Assistance Options from the menu.
    - ✓ Select "Navigation Aids" from the menu.
    - ✓ The "Taxi Ribbon" should be set to "On."
    - ✓ The "Landing Assist/Guide" should be set to "Off" to avoid any conflicts.
  - **Progressive Taxi:** Directions to gates or parking are shown by a dotted line. To activate it:
    - ✓ Launch the window for ATC.
    - ✓ Pick "Progressive Taxi" as your choice.

- **Taking a taxi to the gate:** Once help features are activated, do the following actions:
  - **Adhere to the Taxi Ribbon:** To negotiate the taxiways, use the blue dotted line as a guide. Depending on the size and volume of traffic at the airport, keep your speed within a safe range, usually 10 to 20 knots.
  - **Comply with ATC directions:** Always heed Ground Control's directions. When you speak with Ground Control, ask for a particular gate assignment if you haven't been granted one.
  - **Keep an eye out for airport signs:** To be sure you are headed in the right direction, heed taxiway signs and markings. This is particularly true for big airports with many of taxiways that cross across.

- **Parking at the Gate:** When you reach the gate you have been assigned:
  - **Align with the Gate:** Properly place your aircraft within the gate area using the in-game map or charts.
  - **Request Pushback:** Ask Ground Control for pushback if your aircraft is pointing in the incorrect direction.
  - **Shut down Engines:** After parking the aircraft correctly, shut down the engines and finish the post-flight procedures by following the checklist.

- **Solving Typical Problems:** If navigating a cab is difficult for you:

- ➢ **Taxi Ribbon Not Appearing:** Verify that Taxi Ribbon is enabled by opening Assistance Options. Switch off and then back on the Taxi Ribbon.
- ➢ **ATC Is Not Giving Me Taxi directions:** If Ground Control isn't giving you taxi directions, ask for them yourself. Update the software or restart your Sim if this doesn't work.
- ➢ **Problems with Gate Assignment:** Ask Ground Control for an allocated gate if you don't already have one. Make sure your aircraft type is suitable with the gate size and that the arriving airport has open gates.
- ✦ **Improved Experience:** To make the experience even better:
  - ➢ **Use Airport Charts:** To familiarize yourself with an airport's overall layout, use real-world airport charts. This improves realism and facilitates navigation.
  - ➢ **Install Add-ons:** To enhance the visual appeal and precision of airport layouts, think about adding intricate airport sceneries.
  - ➢ **Practice Often:** You will become more adept at gate operations and taxiing if you practice often at various airports.

Turning Off the Aircraft

In addition to protecting the virtual aircraft's equipment, a proper shutdown makes your simulation experience more realistic.

- ✦ **Finishing the taxi ride and landing at the parking lot:** Once your approach and landing are successful, taxi your plane to the parking lot. Maintain situational awareness, adhere to regular taxi procedures, and contact virtual ATC as necessary.
- ✦ **Parking and Applying the Brake:** To avoid any unwanted movement, align the aircraft correctly and apply the parking brake once it is in the parking position.
- ✦ **Turning Off the Engines:** Depending on the kind of engine, the shutdown process varies:
  - ➢ **Jet engines:**
    - ✓ Press CTRL + SHIFT + F1 in MSFS 2024 to turn off jet engines.
  - ➢ **Engines with pistons:**
    - ✓ Turn the throttle down to idle.
    - ✓ Turn off the engines' fuel mixture.
    - ✓ Switch the magnetos off.
    - ✓ Turn off the gasoline pumps.

In MSFS 2024, these procedures are typically applicable to a variety of aircraft types.

- ✦ **Shutdown of Electrical Systems:** Turn off all electrical systems as soon as the engines have stopped:
  - ➢ Turn off the lights and avionics.

➢ Turn off the alternator and batteries by clicking their switches.
✦ **Protecting the Aircraft:** To finish the shutdown:
➢ The 'off' setting on the parking brake should be clicked.
➢ Every door and hatch has to be shut.
➢ Press the exterior view or virtual cockpit buttons to exit the airplane.

CHAPTER TEN
THE MISSIONS AND CAREER MODE

Examining Potential Career Modes

In Career Mode, MSFS 2024 provides a large number of missions that are reminiscent to actual aircraft tasks. More than 3 million procedurally generated actions from all around the globe are included in this edition alone, including air search and rescue, firefighting and agricultural missions.

Types of Missions

The Career Mode provides a variety of task types with varying rewards and challenges:

- **Agricultural Flights:** Using farming expertise, precisely dust crops and provide other agricultural services.
- **Firefighting:** Take part in aircraft firefighting, which involves putting water or retardants on flames.
- **Air Search and Rescue:** Take part in finding and saving individuals in various situations.
- **Air ambulance:** Delivers patients back to hospitals with a focus on safety and speed.
- **VIP Transportation:** Executive travel requires discretion and timeliness.
- **Cargo transport:** Use scheduling and logistics management to deliver items to several locations.
- **Air Racing:** Take part in fast-paced races against other accomplished pilots.
- **Experimental Aircraft Testing:** To assist manufacturers in gathering crucial data, test new types of aircraft.
- **Mountain Rescue:** Rescue individuals from mountainous regions by flying across challenging terrain.
- **Skydiving:** Drop off skydivers at precise places where time and precision are crucial.
- **Weather Reconnaissance:** Gather important information on weather trends to aid meteorologists.
- **Outsized Cargo Transport:** Like the Airbus Beluga, large cargo may be transported in enormous quantities. Anywhere and anywhere.
- **Arctic Cargo Transport:** Deliver goods to arctic or polar areas.

Advancement and Accreditation

Only after gaining certain certified talents may players access certain tasks. The player will acquire the abilities required to complete challenging tasks as a result of the growth. For instance, the player must complete training modules and performance exams before to taking on a firefighting mission.

System of Dynamic Missions

The dynamic mission system in MSFS 2024 is updated every day with fresh possibilities and challenges. Because new tasks are constantly being introduced, the experience is kept interesting and there's always something new to accomplish.

Worldwide Employment Possibilities

This career mode is worldwide in nature rather than regionally limited. Traveling about the globe and experiencing its many regions, each with its own goals and difficulties, is possible. This gives the game a global perspective and offers a lot of gameplay diversity.

Challenges Every Week & Photographer Mode

Together with the Career Mode, MSFS 2024 also adds a new Weekly Challenge Mode where players will take part in weekly missions and situations. Players will be forced to test their abilities in a variety of aircraft and settings in this mode. The new Photographer Mode adds a creative element to the simulation by allowing players to take pictures of certain in-game places.

Improved Environmental Features and Realism

The MSFS 2024 may provide more visual detail in landing locations for more realism thanks to improved ground landscape creation. Wildfires, snow, tornadoes, auroras, animal migration and herds, live marine and air monitoring, the four seasons, and improved ground traffic reporting are some of the other new features. These enhance immersion and will further enhance the simulator's realism.

Taking Part in Rescue and Search Operations

SAR-related missions in MSFS 2024 are often related to locating individuals in trouble and transporting them to a safe location, sometimes in dangerous or inaccessible places. It is possible to have the players look for a missing individual in mountains, deserts, or dense woods. Finding them and bringing them to a secure area is the ultimate goal.

Search and Rescue Mission Unlocking

There are requirements that must be met in order to launch SAR missions in career mode. The need to land on ten bush strips or soft runways is one of them. As may be anticipated during a SAR mission, this guarantees that the player gets experience flying in a variety of terrains and circumstances.

Getting Ready for a Search and Rescue Operation

Before embarking on a SAR expedition, the following actions are strongly advised:

- **Aircraft Selection:** A plane will be chosen for the mission. Although both helicopters and fixed-wing aircraft may be used, helicopters are often employed in these operations due to their ability to hover and land in tight locations. Make sure the aircraft has any essential SAR equipment, such as winches or hoists.
- **Configure Navigation:** Configure the aircraft navigation systems to include routes and waypoints unique to SAR. This configuration covers every possible region and aids in efficient search patterns.
- **Assignment Briefing:** Go over the specifics of the assignment, such as the search area, the climate, and any known dangers. Planning the search approach requires an understanding of the terrain and possible impediments.

Performing the Search

Following the start of the mission, the following procedures are typically followed:

- **Search Pattern:** An appropriate, consistent search pattern that covers the region being searched, such as a grid or expanding square. For optimal visibility and detecting capabilities, adjust speed and altitude.
- **Detection:** Look for any indications of trouble, such as smoke, signals, or real visual sightings, using all onboard sensors, visual observation, and all accessible information.
- **Awareness:** The aircrew evaluates to decide on the proper response after identifying a target that could be in trouble. Coordination with other aircraft or ground teams may be required for this.

Rescue Activities

Following the recovery of the missing individuals, the rescue process includes the following:

+ **Approach:** A strategy for reaching the rescue location that takes wind, weather, and geography into account.
+ **Rescue Technique:** Depending on the aircraft and mission needs, this technique entails lifting, winching, or landing the aircraft in order to raise the people.
+ **Transportation:** Deliver the rescued individuals to the secure location while taking precautions for their wellbeing.

Obstacles and Things to Think About

In MSFS 2024, SAR faces the following difficulties:

+ **Terrain and Weather:** Operation requires expertise and flexibility in a variety of terrains and weather situations.
+ **Aircraft Limitations:** Every aircraft has both strengths and weaknesses. Comprehending them will be essential to the mission's success.
+ **Operation Complexity:** The search, rescue, and medical evacuation phases of a multistage operation each have their own set of challenges.

Taking Part in Firefighting Activities

A new, comprehensive career option in Microsoft Flight Simulator 2024 exposes players to almost every aspect of aviation, including the vital function of aerial firefighting. Players will be able to construct a virtual aviation career by completing a variety of missions and earning certificates in this mode's organized progression system.

Aerial Firefighting Missions for MSFS 2024

Aerial firefighting greatly strengthens MSFS 2024's career mode, which is one of its strongest points. From inside the cockpit, players are thrust into actual firefighting situations. The tasks will provide difficulties and demand the duties necessary to fight a wildfire from above.

Mission Goals and Structure

In MSFS 2024, firefighting missions are divided into many mission categories, each with distinct goals:

- **Initial Attack Missions:** Usually deployed to contain minor flames before they spread, these are brief operations. The player has to locate the fire, determine how big it is, and then use the right technique to put it out.
- **Extended Attack Missions:** Due to the size of these flames, a prolonged operation will be necessary. To properly combat the fire, a player may have to coordinate with ground personnel, perform many water drops, and maneuver over challenging terrain.

Equipment and Aircraft

The following are some of the firefighting aircraft that MSFS 2024 will have:

- **Fixed-Wing Aircraft:** Water scoops are installed on the Bombardier 415 and other aircraft to enable rapid water deployment and pickup.
- **Helicopters:** Aircraft like the H145 can carry out operations like water bucket drops and resupply ground personnel when equipped with the proper gear, such as a mission pack. The Action Pack, which includes firefighting variations that may communicate with real-time fire databases to enhance the mission simulation experience, is one example of this for the H145.

Advancement and Accreditation

Players must first get the required certificates in order to take part in firefighting missions:

- **Basic Firefighting Certificate:** This beginning certificate enables players to carry out basic assault tasks.

- **Advanced Firefighting Certificate:** This entails handling intricate situations, such as coordinating emergency services and conducting night operations to execute extended assault missions.

Obstacles and Things to Think About

Even though battling fires is fun, there are a few things to be aware of:
- **Seasonal Availability:** Seasons and regions have a significant role in the firefighting tasks. This only indicates that some areas won't have any active flames over the winter and won't provide the same quests. You can see in-game hotspots by looking at the density map.
- **Assignment Generation:** According to some gamers, no further missions are created after the first firefighting assignment. This may be the result of a problem in the game or just the little amount of missions that are accessible. You could find additional answers or insights by reading the community forums.

Carrying Out Cargo Transport Activities

In MSFS 2024, the career mode will be entertaining and realistic. From agricultural dusting to VIP transportation, it will showcase more than 3 million procedurally created actions throughout the globe. The player will go on missions in this mode in order to pass examinations or get certain credentials; mentors will assist them in overcoming obstacles, and real regional personalities will be portrayed.

Launching Missions for Cargo Transport

From tiny aircraft performing quick local deliveries to huge airliners conducting long-haul cargo flights worldwide, MSFS 2024's cargo transport tasks are broken down by aircraft size and type. Your aircraft must be specially outfitted to participate in these activities. To participate in the fun, your aircraft must fulfill the following requirements:

Requirements for Aircraft

- The navigation_graph_pilot.cfg file has to be on the aircraft.
- It is recommended that the operational state be either "in_service" or "experimental."
- It is not possible to mark the aircraft as premium.
- The ui_max_range of the aircraft must be greater than 1.

Other restrictions for transporting light goods include:

- The ApronWithoutCovers.flt file has to be on the airplane.
- It must be an object of the class "Airplane."
- It is not possible to designate the aircraft as military.
- There cannot be a copilot on the aircraft.
- The mass of the cargo must fall between 35 and 680 kg.
- The volume of the fuselage must exceed 1 m³.
- The aircraft may have wheels or large landing gear wheels.
- Skis or floats for landing gear are not allowed on the aircraft.

The airplane will be suitable for the game's freight transport tasks thanks to these specs.

Finishing Cargo Operations

You will be able to start a freight transport business as you go in career mode. 35,000 bank credits are required to do this: 10,000 to acquire the business and 25,000 to buy a Cessna 172 Skyhawk. You may only attach each aircraft you buy to a single corporation. Once your business is up and running, you may embark on different cargo missions. These enable you to progressively advance to harder tasks since they differ in challenge and reward. Light cargo transportation in small aircraft or substantial freight transportation in large aircraft might be the source of this.

Advice for Cargo Transport Mission Success

- **Getting the Aircraft Ready:**
  - Verify that your aircraft meets the requirements for the planned freight flight.
  - Continue to upgrade your aircraft on a regular basis to enable it to transport larger loads further.
- **Choosing a Mission:**
  - Don't take on missions with your present aircraft specs; instead, work your way up to more difficult ones.
  - Pay special attention to the mission's specifics, such as the weight and destination that your aircraft can handle.
- **Planning a Flight:**

> When planning trips, take fuel consumption, air traffic, and weather into account.
> To improve navigation and flight planning, make use of in-game tools and resources.

⁜ **Effective Time Management:**
> Plan flights in accordance with mission deadlines to ensure on-time delivery.
> Take into account delays brought on by bad weather or other unforeseen circumstances.

Overseeing Professional Development

Beginning Your Career

At debut, MSFS 2024 allows users to design an avatar with a variety of races, haircuts, outfits, and even voices, including their own. The immersive experience is improved by this customisation. To advance in their aviation careers, they begin at any small aero club in the globe and work for an airline. Players begin by learning to fly simple, light aircraft, accumulating flying hours, improving their ratings, and preparing for the necessary test to get a particular license. Preparing an aircraft for flight, starting the engines, taxiing, lift-off, and general flying exercises in controlled air conditions and ascension are all part of its early development.

Advancing Through Specializations and Certifications

In order to advance in your career in MSFS 2024, you must have certain certifications and specializations. A player must get the necessary certification to operate a variety of aircraft, including rotorcraft and fixed-wing aircraft. A variety of tasks in Career Mode call for various certificates. The player may specialize in operating commercial aircraft for the transportation of passengers, freight, or other specialist aviation fields as they advance in the game.

Making Money and Taking Care of It

As the game progresses, players are able to accept several mission types with varying payoffs. A Cessna 172, for instance, may have 40,000 credits each flight hour for light freight trips. However, the cost of buying and maintaining an airplane is high. A secondhand Cessna 208 Caravan, for instance, may cost around two million credits. Affording such an aircraft may need around 100 flying hours when maintenance and relocation are taken into account. Players must carefully manage their profits and spending because of this financial component, which adds a sense of realism.

Ownership of Aircraft and Fleet Administration

Initially, it is possible to obtain insurance and aircraft at a discounted price. However, the player may have to pay a large repair cost or the aircraft may be lost permanently if it is damaged or destroyed. The remaining aircraft are purchased at full price, emphasizing prudent flying and sound financial management.

Obstacles and Things to Think About

Although the Career Mode offers a methodical approach to advancement, users have observed many obstacles in this mode, including the need to grind through ranks and the cost of purchasing and maintaining aircraft. Furthermore, the possibilities for advancing in this mode are severely limited since other objectives, such as large freight transfer, could not function. The gamers are worried about the lack of clarity around the compensation for a task and how it would affect their reputation and future career.

CHAPTER ELEVEN
ENVIRONMENTAL AND WEATHER CONDITIONS
Comprehending Weather Integration in Real Time

A real-time weather system in MSFS 2024 will be able to replicate constantly changing weather conditions in terms of clouds, precipitation, wind patterns, and atmospheric pressure. This will be made possible by the recent collaboration with Meteoblue, a meteorological service that produces very precise predictions by combining more than 40 weather models with in-house artificial intelligence.

Essential Elements of Current Weather

- **Dynamic Weather Patterns:** The simulator simulates the world's cyclical weather, including clear skies, fog, and thunderstorms.
- **Global Coverage:** Pilots can see the atmospheric conditions that await their trip from anywhere in the world thanks to its updated weather conditions.
- **Seasonal Weather:** MSFS 2024 offers users the opportunity to experience a variety of climates and weather patterns throughout the year thanks to its seasonal adjustments.
- **Better visuals:** Accurate cloud development, light, and atmospheric conditions that are close to real-life are some of the visual elements that real-time weather offers.

Performance and Accuracy

The accuracy of MSFS 2024 live weather has been discussed by users. A few of them even compared the weather in simulation and the actual world side by side, pointing out instances when things didn't go as planned. One user, for instance, examined MSFS 2024's live weather and compared it to actual weather conditions and X-Plane 12's live weather feature to highlight any instances in which the simulator's weather representation may not be entirely accurate. Nevertheless, a lot of users think that the live weather is a fantastic addition that finally gives the flight simulation experience even more realism and immersion.

Modifying the Weather Conditions

Because MSFS 2024 is adaptable, customers may configure weather variables to suit their tastes. Pilots have the option to fly in the current weather or alter it to rehearse a particular situation. Training or seeing unusual weather events might benefit from this.

Changing the Weather Scenarios

With its advanced weather and ambient settings, Microsoft Flight Simulator 2024 (MSFS 2024) gives users a more realistic simulation experience. This simulator creates dynamic, real-time weather conditions via its connection to Meteoblue. Many tools and third-party add-ons are available in MSFS 2024 to let users customize the circumstances they wish to replicate in order to create unique weather scenarios.

Customization of the Weather in MSFS 2024

Through its interface, MSFS 2024 lets the user adjust the weather conditions directly. The choices are included in the simulator's weather settings menu, where users may adjust visibility, wind speed, precipitation, and cloud cover. Pilots can navigate through the most severe storms because to this adaptability.

Add-ons from Third Parties for More Customization

Of course, third-party add-ons may be helpful for a more comprehensive and extensive variety of potential weather conditions. SoFly's Weather Preset Pro v2 for MSFS 2024 is one such. With its more than 200 unique settings, which include blizzards, tropical storms, and various cloud formations, users may effortlessly swap between them inside the simulator. Another significant feature is REX Atmos, which has emerged as one of the essential visual enhancing tools for completely revamping the MSFS 2024 virtual environment. It significantly improves lighting, cloud patterns, and atmospheric effects to provide a much more engaging flying experience.

Creating Your Own Weather Situations

Custom weather themes are available in MSFS 2024 for individuals who want to create certain weather conditions. This implies that a specific situation may be simulated by entering the precise meteorological conditions at a certain location and time. Custom scenarios will be based on actual meteorological data because of the link with Meteoblue's data.

Particular Weather Factors

Flight dynamics should be taken into account even if the ability to alter weather conditions enhances the flying experience in flight simulators. Extreme weather, for example, may change an aircraft's overall performance; thus, it will be essential to change flying procedures. Therefore, in order to assure safe and realistic flying, it is crucial to comprehend the various weather conditions.

Changing the Season and Time Settings

With its user-friendly settings, MSFS 2024 makes it simple to adjust the weather, sample various seasons, and vary the time of day.

How to Modify the Daytime

In MSFS 2024, you may alter the time of day by doing the following:
- **Open the menu while in flight:**
  - ➤ After taking off, drag the mouse pointer to the toolbar, which will show up in the upper middle of the screen?
  - ➤ To access the weather and time settings, click the cloud symbol.
- **Time Spent Editing:**
  - ➤ There is a slider in the weather and time dialog named "Time of Day."
  - ➤ Adjust this slider to the desired time.
  - ➤ You may adjust the time to the precise hour and minute if necessary.

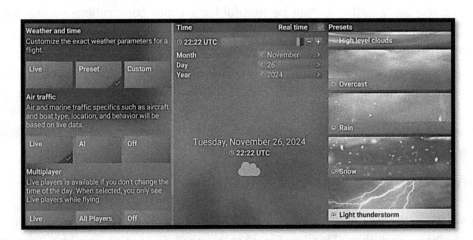

You may experiment with different lighting conditions and circumstances by altering the time during a flight.

Changing Seasonal Preferences

To modify the MSFS 2024 season:
- Getting to the World Map: Prior to the start of the flight, open the World Map.
- Choosing Flight Conditions: Click the generally found "Flight Conditions" box at the top of the screen. Select "Custom."
- Modify Season: Select "Season" from the list of choices that will appear for custom settings. Choose the season of your choosing from the drop-down menu.

You may alter the atmosphere to your preference by changing the season. You may see the splendor of landscapes with blossoming flowers in the spring or experience snow in the winter.

Combining Seasonal and Temporal Changes

It is possible to simultaneously change the time and season in Flight Simulator:
- Open the globe Map: Go to the globe map prior to taking off.
- The second step is to choose the "Flight Conditions" box and select "Custom."
- Changing the Time and Season: You have total control over the "Time of Day" and "Season" in custom.

This enables you to construct a wide range of situations, like a cold evening or a sunny morning.

Extra Advice

- **Current Time and Weather:** Check "Live Weather" and "Live Time" in the weather and time dialog to see the current weather and time. Keep in mind that using live weather sometimes prevents you from manually adjusting the weather parameters.
- **Store your own Presets:** This makes it simpler to set up any specific situation. After you have the time and season selected, store it as your own preset for later use.
- **In-Flight Adjustments:** Keep in mind that you may dynamically alter your surroundings while in flight by adjusting the time using the weather and time dialog.

Understanding the Impact of Weather on Flight Dynamics

The weather modeling inside the platform is much improved by Microsoft Flight Simulator, which also has a deeper effect on flight dynamics. The performance and control of the aircraft are enhanced by a new Computational Fluid Dynamics (CFD) technology, which increases realism while flying through the environment.

Knowing the System of Computational Fluid Dynamics (CFD)

In MSFS 2024, wind and wake turbulence are much more precise, reaching up to 6 minutes in persistence and 10 kilometers surrounding the aircraft. This will enable more realistic mountain flying due to terrain-induced turbulence and updrafts, realistic wake turbulence effects from other aircraft, and enhanced gliding simulation with precise thermal and ridge lift.

Effect on the Dynamics of Flight

Flight dynamics are being significantly impacted by the new CFD technology in a number of ways. Among them are the following:

- **Turbulence Effects:** More realistic and varied turbulence that varies according to weather; more kinds of precipitation, each of which affects aircraft performance differently; enhanced wind effects on flying, landing, and takeoff characteristics; and improved temperature and humidity effects on lift and engine performance.
- **Aircraft Handling:** With realistic thermal and ridge lift, the terrain-induced turbulence modeling and its updrafts provide better gliding and more realistic mountain flight.
- **Icing Conditions:** Adjusting aircraft performance and safety is made possible by more realistic aircraft icing under suitable weather conditions.
- **Water Physics:** When taking off from or landing on water under unfavorable situations, water physics has become more realistic with precise water spray effects.

Novel Weather Events

Completely new weather occurrences are introduced in MSFS 2024, such as:

- **Aurora Borealis:** This adds a visual spectacular to the simulation by allowing players to see the Northern Lights on certain occasions.
- **Tornadoes:** These meteorological phenomena make their debut, are now accessible in some missions, and will soon be included in live events. Ultimately, the engineers are always searching for high-quality materials to enable the live

tornado event. Storm-chasers may face more difficulties as a result of these occurrences.

- ⁜ **Wildfires:** The cloud system has also been modified to provide fog and smoke effects unique to wildfires. This creates difficult firefighting tasks in addition to affecting visibility.

Seasonal Variations and Their Effects

The whole virtual environment undergoes significant changes throughout the year when the seasons are introduced. The shifting seasons are shown in over 23 meticulously designed, very authentic biomes. This will have an impact on flight dynamics, as hot summer weather may create very difficult thermals for glider pilots, while snow and ice can limit takeoff distances and handling.

Simulation of Visibility and Fog

Because of all of that, this feature is much more realistic than its predecessors. It may significantly improve a low-visibility flight simulation and can now depict thin layers of fog or even pollution close to the ground up to elevations of around 2000 meters. It adds more realism and more difficult effects that pilots may not be used to by accurately simulating temperature inversions and visibility problems.

Improved Career Mode and Flight Planning

More sophisticated pre-flight weather briefings are possible because to the flight planner's many more options for checking and customizing weather conditions. For realistic flight planning, forecast weather is linked with the actual weather system and may be observed along planned routes. The dynamic weather system will also be crucial for fans of the career mode. Long-term gameplay will be significantly more realistic and challenging due to the weather, which will also make some objectives accessible or more difficult to complete.

Community Input and Continued Progress

Even though MSFS 2024 has many enhancements, community feedback still indicates that there are still ambiguities. Certain weather elements, such as turbulence during thunderstorms, may not meet the expectations of certain users. Forums like AVSIM and the official MSFS forums are littered with demands for more accurate cloud formation, more realistic turbulence simulation, and more realistic weather interactions. Future updates are anticipated to substantially improve weather effects and flying dynamics and the development team continues to work on such problems. In order to keep MSFS 2024 a dynamic, engaging experience for users, community input greatly influences the simulator's evolution.

Using Tools and Weather Radar

Weather radar is essential for identifying and avoiding dangerous weather conditions including thunderstorms, turbulence, and precipitation in actual aviation. By giving the pilot the resources they need to properly analyze and react to weather, MSFS 2024 attempts to imitate this.

Important Tools and Features

+ **Improved Atmospheric Lighting and Cloud Graphics:** MSFS 2024 has a redesigned cloud rendering engine that adds greater volume and realism to cloud forms. This gives pilots a clearer visual picture of certain weather conditions and potential dangers.
  ➢ To accurately depict light interactions with the atmosphere, the new Atmospheric Lighting Engine makes use of sophisticated ray tracing. This improvement will provide pilots better visual signals about weather conditions to aid in navigation and decision-making.
+ **Novel Weather Events:** There are new meteorological phenomena including tornadoes, wildfires, and the Aurora Borealis. With these enhancements, pilots may fly in a variety of weather situations and the simulation becomes more realistic.
+ **Simulating visibility and fog:** Layers of fog and pollution close to the ground that impair vision up to around 2000 meters above sea level are now correctly modeled by the simulator. Pilots need this functionality in order to anticipate and be ready for poor visibility situations.
+ **Effect on Gameplay and Flight Dynamics:** A new CFD system is included in MSFS 2024 to more accurately model wake and wind turbulence. Realistic wake turbulence effects from other aircraft are made possible by the technology, which lasts up to six minutes and stretches 10 kilometers surrounding the aircraft.

Using Tools and Weather Radar

Follow the steps listed below to make use of MSFS 2024's weather radar and related tools:

+ **Getting Weather Information:** In the simulator, activate the weather radar display by turning it on from the aircraft's avionics panel. This will show the location and intensity of precipitation in almost real-time.

- **Interpret Weather Data:** Recognize the meaning of the colors and intensities seen on the radar: Generally speaking, mild precipitation is represented by green, moderate precipitation by yellow and heavy precipitation by red.
- **Modify the Radar Configuration:** To maximize the display's representation of the real flying circumstances, adjust the gain, tilt, and range. Accurate weather phenomenon identification will be made possible by proper adjustment.
- **Integration with Flight Planning:** To anticipate and steer clear of bad weather, combine weather radar data with flight planning software. Integration improves flying efficiency and safety.

Obstacles and Things to Think About

Despite its sophisticated weather modeling, MSFS 2024 has many drawbacks.

- **Access to Weather Data:** The simulator's weather API mostly functions as an input API for reading weather data, which restricts third-party developers' capacity to design unique weather radar systems and, therefore, the availability of more sophisticated features.
- **Integration with Third-Party Tools:** Due to their restricted APIs, several third-party weather tools, such ActiveSky, have had trouble connecting with MSFS 2024. The availability of improved weather radar features will be impacted.

CHAPTER TWELVE
ONLINE FLYING AND MULTIPLAYER

Configuring Sessions for Multiplayer

To set up multiplayer sessions, follow these steps:

How to Get to the Multiplayer Settings

- **Launch MSFS 2024:** The first step is to start the simulator and go to the main menu.
- **Go to World Map:** To arrange your flight, choose "World Map" from this menu.
- **Open Flight Conditions:** Select "Flight Conditions" from the World Map screen, then go into the Multiplayer settings.

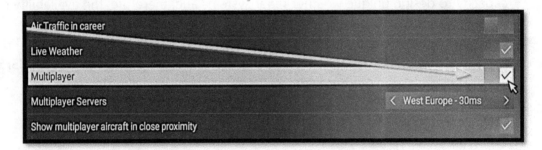

Setting up Multiplayer Preferences

There are many multiplayer options inside the Flight Conditions menu:
- **In multiplayer mode, the following choices are available:**
  - **Live Players:** You may see other players and communicate with those who are online thanks to this option.
  - **All Players:** This will show every player, including those who aren't online right now.
  - **Off:** Disables multiplayer functionality.
- **Server Selection:** Choose any server from this list based on where you are or where you want to travel. The performance and latency would be enhanced if you choose a server that is close to your location.

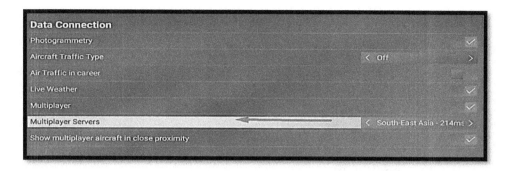

✈ Choose the weather, time of day, and other environmental conditions for your flight.

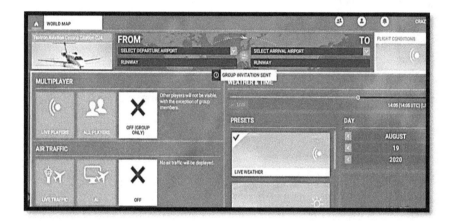

Join or Form a Group

To provide more control and promote more civil multiplayer gaming, MSFS 2024 offers the following options for setting up a private group:

Forming a Group

✈ **Invite Friends:** Go to your friends list and extend an invitation to everyone you would want to have in your group.

✈ **Set Group Leader:** The group's flying conditions may be set by the group leader.

Acquiring Membership in a Group

✈ **Accept Invitations:** If you get an invitation, accept it to join the group.

✈ **Adhere to the group leader's settings:** After joining the group, adhere to the flight parameters that the group leader has established.

Modify the Traffic and Graphics Settings

The following might further enhance the multiplayer experience:
- **Graphics Settings:** Verify that the graphics settings are optimized for performance. If you have a lot of other aircraft in view, turning some of them down could improve fps.
- **Traffic Settings:** You may choose the number of planes you want to observe using AI and real-time traffic settings. Busier skies are the consequence of higher settings; however system performance may be impacted.

Taking Off

After configuring the aforementioned parameters,
- **Return to World Map:** Go back to the World Map when everything has been configured.
- **Pick Your Plane and departing Location:** Decide on your preferred aircraft and departing point.
- **Launch:** Press "Fly" to launch into multiplayer flight.

Multiplayer Interactions in Flight

You and other multiplayer players may accomplish the following while in flight:
- **Communicate:** Use voice chat inside the game or third-party communication platforms to speak with other players.
- **Flight Plan:** To ensure that the flights are coordinated, share your flight plan with the other members of your party.
- **Events:** Take part in group flights created by other players or community gatherings.

Troubleshooting Typical Issues

If you're experiencing issues with multiplayer:
- **Server Connection:** Verify that the server you are attempting to reach is operational.
- **Visibility:** Verify that you are on the same mode or server as your friends in the multiplayer settings if you are not visible to others.
- **Performance:** Try modifying traffic and graphics settings for a good performance vs. visual balance if multiplayer performance suffers.

Getting Involved in Online Communities

Both virtual and actual pilots may join MSFS 2024 online forums to exchange experiences, take part in group flights, and talk about different facets of flight simulation. You may locate individuals to work with and learn from by using these forums, social media groups, or even specific locations.

The Advantages of Participating in Online Communities

- **Shared Learning and Support:** Engaging with seasoned pilots can help you accelerate your learning curve. Tutorials, troubleshooting hints, and even pointers on advanced flying methods have been offered by several forums.
- **Participation in Group Flights:** A lot of places have frequent group flights where you may practice formation flying, take part in coordinated flying, and go to new places with other people.
- **Access to Exclusive Content:** Members exchange unique missions, scenery, and aircraft that enhance the simulator experience beyond what is available.
- **Networking Opportunities:** Get to know others, create lifelong friendships, and sometimes locate collaborators for a variety of flight simulation projects.

Well-known Online Communities for MSFS 2024

- One of the largest websites for flight simulation is AVSIM. In 1996, it was introduced. The website offers product reviews, download libraries, and forums. It serves as a gathering place for MSFS users to exchange materials and have discussions.
- **VFHUB:** Virtual flight is the main emphasis of this community. They provide pilots a place to interact, exchange stories, and take part in group flights. In order to communicate in real time, they also keep up a Discord server.
- One of the most popular subreddits on Reddit is r/MicrosoftFlightSim, where users may exchange screenshots, debate various MSFS topics, and share their experiences. An excellent resource for guidance or news updates.
- **Discord Servers:** A lot of communities keep up Discord servers that facilitate resource sharing, group flight planning, and real-time communication. There is an example of an active VFHUB Discord server that welcomes new users.

How to Sign Up and Take Part

- **Join Forums:** Join community forums like AVSIM, read conversations, make use of the tools provided, and stay informed about forthcoming events.

- **Joining Discord Servers:** Use an invite link to join a Discord server. Engage in voice and text conversations, take part in group flights, and assist in completing existing tasks.
- **Attend Virtual Events:** It's well known that many communities have frequent events, such as tournaments, challenges, and group flights. To become involved in the community and hone your talents, go to these events.
- **Provide Content:** You may contribute to the community by writing about your experience, making a lesson, or designing your own aircraft or scenery.

Tips for Effective Participation

- **Be Courteous and Respectful:** Treat people with courtesy at all times; a cheerful disposition will make the community more welcoming to everyone.
- **Stay Current:** Pay attention to debates, events, and fresh information on the community platforms.
- **Ask Questions and receive Help When Needed:** The community is here to help, so don't be afraid to ask questions and receive support when you need it.
- **Share Your Experiences:** To improve the community, share screenshots, your flying experiences, and your thoughts.

Interaction with Other Pilots

Pilots from all around the globe may engage, connect, and share the sky with MSFS 2024's rich multiplayer flying features. For virtual flights to be coordinated, safe, and more realistic, communication will be crucial.

Features for In-Game Communication

The following communication tools will be used by MSFS 2024 to facilitate pilot interactions:

- **Voice Chat:** Flyers may converse with others around them using the simulator's in-game voice chat feature. This facilitates experience sharing and group flight planning.
- **Text Chat:** Pilots may send messages to individuals or groups using MSFS 2024's in-game chat tool, which is ideal for those who prefer a text-based approach. This makes it simpler to share queries or information without relying on third-party apps.
- **Radio Frequencies:** Pilots may use the simulator to listen in to certain radio frequencies in order to speak with nearby aircraft. Any simulation is made more realistic by the simulator, which allows pilots to converse over the radio, much as in real life.

Configuring and Making Use of Communication Tools

To use these features for communication:

- **Getting into Multiplayer Mode:** From the main menu, choose the World Map tab. In the upper-right area, there is a drop-down choice labeled "Air Traffic." Choose "Multiplayer" to access the shared virtual world.
- To activate Voice Chat, configure your microphone in the simulator's settings. Voice chat must to be on by default when you go to multiplayer mode. To ensure clear communication, adjust the sensitivity and loudness settings appropriately.
- **Text Chatting:** The chat window is typically opened by using the Enter key. After typing, press "Enter" to send the message. All players or the players of one are choosing get messages.
- **Radio Frequency Tuning:** The required frequency may be adjusted using on-cockpit radio controls. Similar to actual radio conversations, this makes it possible to converse with other pilots at that frequency and is quite realistic.

Tools for Third-Party Communication

Even though MSFS 2024 offers a number of in-game interfaces, some pilots choose to use third-party apps that enhance functionality. **It will have the following benefits or attributes:**

- **Discord:** Pilots may establish servers and channels for certain flights or groups using this voice and text application. It is popular among flight simulator clubs and provides excellent voice chat quality.

- **TeamSpeak:** This dependable and low-latency group communication tool is also available. Additionally, it provides capabilities that meet various communication needs, such as customized channels and push-to-talk.
- **SayIntentions.AI:** This AI-powered air traffic control system uses speech recognition to enhance real-time communication. In addition to supporting various flight types, it can integrate with MSFS 2024 to provide an even more dynamic and realistic communication channel.

Top Techniques for Clear Communication

In order to guarantee seamless and efficient communication during multiplayer sessions:
- **Clarity and Brevity:** When communicating, use language that is both clear and succinct. To make sure everyone understands, stay away from superfluous jargon.
- **Situational Awareness:** Pay attention to your surroundings and other planes' whereabouts. This awareness aids in conflict avoidance and movement coordination.
- **Professionalism and Courtesy:** Always communicate in a courteous manner. Everyone's experience is improved overall by this professionalism.
- **Standard Procedures:** Learn about the accepted practices for aviation communication. Understanding normal operating procedures would maintain interactions' effectiveness and realism.

Problems and Issues

Even if MSFS 2024 is a great communications tool, the following items might cause problems:
- **Technical Issues:** Voice chat may sometimes have latency or connectivity issues. Those issues are probably caused by the internet; modify the settings to get the best results.
- **Privacy Concerns:** Always pay attention to the permissions and privacy settings while using third-party applications. Make sure the information you are offering makes you feel at ease.
- **Learning Curve:** At first, new users can find the communication tools confusing. To become competent, you must practice and grow accustomed to it.

Taking Part in Flights in Groups

Pilots may share the sky, visit new places together, and take part in coordinated aviation events by flying in groups.

Configuring Multiplayer for Flights in Groups

To guarantee a flawless experience, it's crucial to set up your multiplayer settings before joining group flights. **Take these actions:**

- Go to the World Map after launching MSFS 2024 to see the multiplayer settings. After selecting the "General" option, choose "Online."
- **Configure Multiplayer Options:** To see every online participant, set "Multiplayer" to "All Players". Select a server area that is close to your location and delivers the best performance. Adjust the "Air Traffic" parameters to your liking, but be advised that excessive levels may result in subpar performance.
- **Set Flight Conditions:** To ensure constant weather and time settings, choose "Preset" under "Flight Conditions." Avoid using "Live" on the weather and time since this might cause the multiplayer settings to return to "Live Players," which would make other players less visible.

By using these, you would have set up your multiplayer settings for a fantastic group flight.

Locating and Participating in Group Flight Activities

MSFS 2024 often hosts group flights and has a vibrant community. To locate and participate in such events:

- **Examine Community Events:** Look for forthcoming community gatherings and group flights in the "Community Events" section of the official Microsoft Flight Simulator forums.
- **Join Virtual Aviation Communities:** Use Facebook and Discord to connect with virtual aviation communities. For example, the "Bush Divers" club often organizes group flights, particularly for pilots of low and slow aircraft.
- **Participate in a Scheduled Fly-In:** There is a number of planned fly-ins in various towns, such "Community Fly-In Friday," when participants often take a weekly flight to a new location.
- **Working Title Flight Planner:** For simpler group flying, MSFS 2024 includes new online companion software from Working Title that enables you to make and share flight plans with your buddies.

Take Part in Group Flights

To join a group flying event, locate it and do the following actions:
- **Participate in the Event:**
  - Use the community's preferred event platform, such as Facebook, Discord, or another one, to RSVP or register for the event.

- You may need to download specific flight plans or aircraft models for certain events.
- **Get your aircraft ready:**
  - Make sure your selected aircraft and any necessary add-ons are ready.
  - Go over the flight plan and familiarize yourself with any particular route protocols.
- **Take Part in the Multiplayer Game:**
  - Launch MSFS 2024 and load the intended route at the appointed time.
  - Use the server address and configuration provided by the event hosts to join the multiplayer session.
- **Interaction with Other Pilots:**
  - Make use of your choice external communication tool, like Discord, or voice chat inside the game.
  - To guarantee a seamless event, follow all established communication guidelines.

How to Make Your Group Flight Great

- **Stay Informed:** Pay attention to social media groups and community forums for updates on forthcoming events and group flights.
- **Involve the Community:** To improve your flying experience, take part in conversations, exchange stories, and make contributions to the community.
- **Be Ready:** To guarantee a seamless experience, familiarize yourself with the flight schedule, aircraft, and any special protocols before to the event.
- **Observe Event Guidelines:** Adhere to the rules and regulations set out by the event planners to guarantee a satisfying experience for each and every participant.

Controlling the Multiplayer Configuration

Flying will be smooth and pleasurable if the parameters are managed properly.

Turning on Multiplayer Capabilities

To begin with, make sure that the multiplayer feature is turned on:
- Use the main menu to access the settings, then choose "Options."
- On the "General" menu, choose "Data." Then, select "Online Functionality" and make sure it is turned on.
- Turn Multiplayer On: Toggle "Multiplayer" to On under the same "Data" section.

To interact with other pilots, all of them require ensuring that the multiplayer features are on.

Choosing a Server

Your multiplayer experience will be greatly improved by selecting the right server:
- On the main menu, choose "World Map."
- Click on your login in the upper right corner to choose a server. There will be a list of servers that are available. Choose a server based on your preferred activity level and geographic location.

By picking a server near you, you may lower latency and increase connection reliability.

Setting up Traffic Settings

The presence and actions of other aircraft are determined by modifying the traffic settings:
- **Access Traffic Settings:** Click "Filters" under "World Map" to access traffic settings.
- **Configure Aircraft Traffic Type:** From the "Aircraft Traffic Type," choose one of the options below:
  - **Off:** Only your aircraft will be visible.
  - **AI Traffic:** The game's artificial intelligence pilots the planes, creating a crowded landscape.
  - **Real-Time Online:** A list of other players' real aircraft movements.
  - Choose "Real-Time Online" to experience a dynamic and engaging situation. However, keep in mind that your network may load more of this.

Aircraft Management Display

To alter the display of other aircraft:
- Navigate to General Settings by choosing "Options," followed by "General."
- Adjust planes Display: Under "Traffic," you may toggle "Use Generic Plane Models (Multiplayer)" to "On" or "Off." "On" utilizes generic models, while "Off" shows planes with their real models.

Performance is enhanced by generic models, particularly on low-end computers.

Configuring the Flight Environment

The realistic flying experience is enhanced by having flight circumstances that are comparable to those of other pilots.
- **Open Flight Conditions:** Select "Flight Conditions" from the "World Map."

- **Modify Weather and Time:** To synchronize with other players, set "Weather" and "Time" to "Preset".
- **Configure Multiplayer Settings:** To see all pilots, independent of their settings, choose "All Players" under "Multiplayer." Use caution since this might show players in varied time and weather conditions, which could detract from realism.

Coordinating weather and timing parameters with other pilots is recommended for a reliable experience.

Handling Real-Time Weather and Time

When live weather is enabled in MSFS 2024, multiplayer settings may be automatically adjusted:
- **Live Weather:** When live weather is enabled, the "Multiplayer" option may be changed to "Live Players," preventing anybody else from seeing it. Set "Multiplayer" to "All Players" and manually modify the weather parameters to keep everyone visible.

Fixing Multiplayer Visibility Issues

If other players are not visible:
- To check the multiplayer settings, make sure that "Multiplayer" is set to "On" under "General" > "Data."
- Verify that the "Aircraft Traffic Type" option is set to "Real-Time Online."
- Alter Aircraft show: Depending on how big of an effect it has on performance, you may either show real aircraft models or generic ones.

Keep in mind that visibility in multiplayer mode may be impacted by network performance. A robust and fast network connection is necessary for optimal performance.

CHAPTER THIRTEEN

PERSONALIZING THE FLIGHT EXPERIENCE

Setting Up Mods and Add-Ons

Mods and add-ons are third-party or user-generated material designed to improve MSFS 2024's functionality. **These may consist of the following:**

- **Aircraft:** Brand-new aircraft with intricate flight dynamics and modeling.
- **Scenery:** New or improved landscape, landmarks, and airports.
- **Utilities:** Instruments that increase functionality, such weather forecasting or flight planners.
- **Missions & Challenges:** Personalized situations and tasks that put your flying prowess to the test.

Finding the Community Folder

Add-ons are usually installed under the Community folder in MSFS 2024. The simulator searches for more information in this directory. **To locate it:**

- Launch MSFS 2024.
- Visit a marketplace.
- Press "My Library."
- Select the "Settings" option next to the search box.
- Select "Open" to see the Community folder's location.

As an alternative, you may choose "Browse" and choose a different directory to move the Community folder.

Marketplace Add-Ons installations

You may purchase and download add-ons directly from MSFS 2024's integrated marketplace:

- Launch the simulator's Marketplace.
- Look for the add-ons you want.
- Once the add-on has been chosen, click "Buy" or "Download."
- The Community folder will automatically install the add-on when it has been downloaded.

To control these add-ons, download updates, turn them on, or turn them off:

- Open Marketplace and go to My Library.
- Choose the Community.
- You can see and control all of your add-ons here.

Installing Add-Ons from Third Parties

For instance, third-party websites that sell add-ons purchased outside of Marketplace adhere to the steps listed below:
- Get the add-on file, which is often in ZIP format.
- Extract the ZIP file's contents.
- Inside the Community folder, put the extracted folder.

To prevent any issues, make sure the add-on is compatible with MSFS 2024.

Handling Mods and Add-Ons

To properly handle your add-ons:
- **Enable or Disable Add-Ons:** Add-ons may be enabled or disabled under "My Library's" "Community" section.
- **Update Add-Ons:** To ensure compatibility and functioning, updates are sometimes made available via the Marketplace or the add-on's source.
- **Disable Add-Ons:** To remove an add-on, remove its folder from the Community directory.

Using Custom Content with the SDK

The SDK is a comprehensive collection of materials and tools that enables users to develop MSFS 2024 add-ons. Editors, compilers, and other documentation are included to let you create your own material. The SDK mostly operates independently of the MSFS 2024 executable. This makes it simple for add-on developers to test and integrate their products.

117

Configuring the SDK

Let's first confirm that the SDK is installed and configured properly:

- **Installation:** The MSFS 2024 installation procedure makes the SDK accessible. It may be downloaded from the official MSFS website or accessible via Developer mode inside the simulator.
- **Developer Mode:** The user must enable Developer Mode in MSFS 2024 in order to utilize SDK tools. Go to the 'Options' menu, choose 'Developer Mode,' and then restart the simulator.
- **Community Folder:** The 'Community' folder is where custom material is kept. To properly manage your add-ons, locate this directory.

Producing Original Content

Objects, scenery, and planes are just a few of the unique content kinds that may be created using the SDK.

- **Custom Items:**
  - **Modeling:** To produce models, use 3D modeling software such as Blender. Make that the models meet the requirements of MSFS 2024 and are performance-optimized.
  - **Exporting:** MSFS 2024 enables exporting models in the glTF format. To preserve the integrity of the model, use the proper export settings.
  - **Integration:** Use Project Editor to import models into the SDK. In this case, it is necessary to establish asset groups and build models into simulator packages.
- **Scenery**
  - **Design:** Use the Scenery Editor to position items and specify their features to create unique scenery components, such as landmarks, airports, or changes to the landscape.
  - **Texturing:** Use the Material Editor to apply texturing to the models. Textures need to be compatible with the MSFS 2024 rendering technology and optimized for it.
  - **Compiling:** The Package Tool may be used to compile scenery projects, and the packages that are produced are accessible from inside the simulator under the 'Community' folder.
- **Aircraft:**
  - **Modeling and Texturing:** This will include modeling and texturing aircraft while taking into account flight dynamics and cockpit features, as well as the MSFS 2024 standard.

- ➢ **Configurations:** This entails using configuration files to build up aircraft behaviors and systems; the SimObject Editor will allow for the improvement of flight models and interfaces.
- ➢ **Testing:** To guarantee precise performance and functionality, thoroughly test aircraft in the simulator.

Top Techniques

The following recommended practices should be taken into account while producing original material for MSFS 2024:
- ✦ **Optimization:** To preserve simulator speed, make sure models and textures are optimized.
- ✦ **Testing:** To find and fix problems quickly, test simulator add-ons on a regular basis.
- ✦ **Documentation:** To promote community cooperation and future upgrades, keep your projects' documentation clear.
- ✦ **Community Contributions:** Make use of the MSFS 2024 communities to spread knowledge, engage with others, and strengthen the ecosystem.

Modifying the Simulation Configuration

This will be crucial for experience customization as well as performance optimization.
- ✦ **Getting to the Simulation Settings:** In MSFS 2024, you can begin customizing the flying experience by going to the settings menu and selecting General settings. There are several categories here, and many more are grouped together, such as the settings for the Graphics, Controls, Camera, and Sound sections in particular.
- ✦ **Visual Settings:** You may adjust a number of visual elements in the "Graphics" area to improve performance and realism.
  - ➢ **Resolution and Display Mode:** Select between windowed, borderless, or full-screen window modes. For optimal clarity, set the resolution to the native resolution of your display.
  - ➢ **V-Sync:** On/off vertical synchronization. While turning off V-Sync can improve performance, it may also cause screen tearing.
  - ➢ **Frame Rate Limiter:** This maintains performance by setting a target frame rate. For improved stability, MSFS 2024 dynamically modifies the parameters to achieve the desired frame rate.

- ➢ **Graphics Presets:** Select from Ultra, High, Medium, or Low. These preset settings provide a compromise between performance and visual accuracy by changing many variables simultaneously.
- ➢ **Advanced Settings:** Enhance the quality of settings like texture, anti-aliasing, shadows, and landscape detail for more precise adjustments. For PCs with inferior performance, they may be lowered or turned off.
- ✦ **Control Settings:** Adjusting the control settings enables responsiveness and comfort while flying:
  - ➢ **Control Profiles:** Establish and maintain profiles for a range of controllers, such as throttle quadrants, joysticks, and yokes. For those who utilize many different controllers, this capability is incredibly beneficial.
  - ➢ **Sensitivity and Dead Zones:** To get the best response, each axis's sensitivity curves and dead zones may be modified. For instance, adjusting the Xbox controller's reactivity settings might result in very precise control.
  - ➢ **Control Assignments:** Assigning buttons, switches, and axes to various purposes. Because MSFS 2024 has extensive lists of commands, anything may be customized.
  - ➢ **Importing Control Profiles:** Despite the addition of new commands in MSFS 2024, customers moving from MSFS 2020 cannot theoretically import their old control schemes. There isn't a method to move settings across versions at the moment.
- ✦ **Camera Settings:** Adjust the camera settings for improved comfort and situational awareness while flying:
  - ➢ **Cockpit Camera:** Adjust the location, angle, and zoom level of the pilot's perspective. It makes it possible to see the cockpit instruments in a comfortable and natural way.
  - ➢ **External Camera:** Use orbital, fly-by, and pursue cameras to position external viewpoints. These views are excellent for dramatic shots and are helpful for monitoring airplanes from various perspectives.
  - ➢ **Camera Presets:** Store personalized camera angles for easy access while flying. Pilots who like certain views during various flying stages may find this option extremely helpful.
- ✦ **Sound Settings: Adjust the sound to your preference:**
  - ➢ **Master Volume:** Modify the overall volume of the sound.
  - ➢ **Speech and Music:** Manage the volume of all in-game speech and music, including ATC messages.
  - ➢ **Environmental Sounds:** Adjust the volume for the sounds of the engine, the weather, and the atmosphere in the cockpit.

- **Accessibility options:** The MSFS 2024 may be used with various types of accessibility thanks to the options shown below.
  - ➢ **Colorblind Modes:** Modification of color based on limitations in color vision.
  - ➢ **Subtitles:** This feature activates the in-game ATC and subtitles for all speech.
  - ➢ **Control Assistance:** Adjust the degree of help provided by navigation, controls, and other flying aids.
- **Performance Optimization:** For MSFS 2024 to operate at its peak, the following factors should be taken into account:
  - ➢ **Hardware:** Use hardware with a respectable CPU, GPU, and sufficient RAM, or at least more than the minimum recommended for MSFS 2024.
  - ➢ **Graphics Settings:** Modify the graphics settings to strike a balance between performance and visual accuracy. Make use of the dynamic graphics function, which modifies settings automatically based on the performance of your machine.
  - ➢ **Background Applications:** To save up system resources, shut off any unused background apps.
  - ➢ **Update Frequently:** Frequently, MSFS 2024 and new graphics driver upgrades include a number of bug fixes and improvements.

Developing custom scenarios

The ability to construct unique scenarios in MSFS 2024 enables the user to customize a particular flying experience according to variables like weather, time of day, aircraft type, and flight routes. This is a very useful tool that can be used for training, evaluating the operation of the aircraft under various situations, or just taking a trip that interests you.

Ways to Develop a Custom Scenario

In MSFS 2024, do the following actions to build a custom scenario:
- **Open the World Map:** Launch MSFS 2024 and go to the World Map, the primary flight planning center.
- **Select the Airports of Arrival and Departure:** To determine the beginning place, click on the departing airport. To find the destination, click on the airport of arrival.
- **Adjust the Flight Settings:**
  - ➢ **Planes Selection:** The user may choose from a variety of available planes.
  - ➢ **Weather Settings:** To provide the necessary difficulties or the best flying circumstances, adjust the weather by displaying wind speed, visibility, and precipitation.

- ➢ **Time of Day:** Configure the date and time to fly in various atmospheric and light conditions.
- ➢ **Flight Plan:** Select airways to fly on, modify itineraries, and add waypoints.
- ✦ **Preserve the Situation:** Save the scenario for later use after all the parameters have been adjusted. This will allow you to easily retrieve your personalized flying settings.

Superior Personalization

Custom missions and challenges may be made in MSFS 2024 for those who want more intricate customizing. This entails creating intricate scenarios with precise goals, events, and circumstances by scripting and using the simulator's SDK, or Software Development Kit, to the fullest. It may be necessary to acquire scripting languages and programming tools in order to use the MSFS 2024 SDK, which calls for a greater understanding of the simulator's internal operations.

Advice for Successful Personalization

- ✦ **Experimentation:** To learn how each parameter impacts the flying experience, don't be scared to try out various settings.
- ✦ **Documentation:** To monitor your preferences and advancements, maintain a record of your customized situations, complete with settings and goals.
- ✦ **Community Involvement:** Take part in community conversations to share your works and get insight from others' experiences.

Distributing Content to the Community

The 'Community' category serves as the foundation for MSFS 2024's main modifications, allowing users to add third-party material like as utilities, scenery, and aircraft. This makes it possible to integrate user-made or downloadable add-ons with ease, extending the simulator's functionality. Pasting the path %LOCALAPPDATA% into Windows File Explorer's address bar will open this folder. Please be aware that %LOCALAPPDATA% may change based on your installation and system setup. For example, some people have said that C:\people\[YourUsername]\AppData\Roaming\ is where their Community folder is.Flight Simulator 2024 by Microsoft. You may relocate the Community folder in MSFS 2024 if you want to keep your add-ons on another disk or directory. Either the UserCfg.opt file or the simulator's settings may be used to do this.

Distributing Content to the Community

It's simple to share your downloaded material and creations with the MSFS community:

 + **Create or Download Add-ons:** You have the option to either make your own add-ons or get them from reliable sources.
 + **Place in Community Folder:** The add-on files must then be placed inside the Community folder.
 + **Share with Others:** To share, just submit your add-ons to community websites such as FlightSim.com or AVSIM. These websites provide a platform for sharing and downloading add-ons since they feature user-generated material.

Make sure you have permission to share material and that your add-ons abide by the hosting platform's community standards.

Platforms for Community Sharing

A number of sites provide ways to obtain and distribute MSFS 2024 content:

 + **AVSIM:** A non-profit social networking site devoted to Microsoft Flight Simulator and flight simulation. The service offers product reviews, a file repository, and a community forum.
 + **FlightSim.com:** A review and resource website for flight simulators that offers users details and accessories for the flight simulator video game franchise.
 + **Microsoft Flight Simulator Forums:** An official collection of forums where users exchange material, talk about the simulator generally, and receive help.

In addition to facilitating the sharing of user-generated content, these platforms provide community events, conversations, and troubleshooting.

CHAPTER FOURTEEN

TECHNIQUES FOR ADVANCED FLIGHT

Executing Operations under Instrument Flight Rules (IFR)

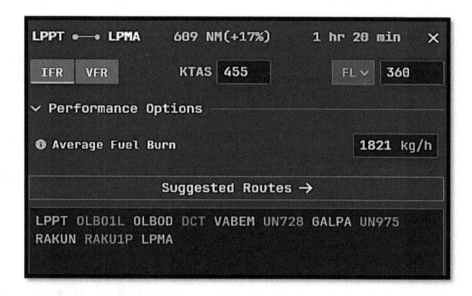

When the weather falls below VFR minimums, Instrument Flight Rules (IFR) operations are conducted. It is necessary to navigate and control the aircraft primarily using flight instruments in weather conditions below these minimums. **Air traffic control (ATC) instructions and radio navigation aids (navaids) are used to complete navigation.**

- **Planning for Flight:** In any IFR, flight planning is still crucial. For creating IFR flight plans, MSFS 2024 has an easy-to-use in-game flight planner:
  - ➤ **Get the Flight Planner here:** Choose your departing and destination airports by opening the World Map.
  - ➤ **Draft an IFR flight schedule:** Enter your route and choose 'IFR' as the flight type under the 'Flight Plan' option. The available airways and waypoints will be used by the simulator to create a route.
  - ➤ **Examining the Path:** To ensure it meets your desired path and does not contravene any airspace limitations, verify the route prepared for waypoints, airways, and elevations.

- ➢ **Weather:** Verify if the conditions are appropriate for IFR operations at the airports where you are departing and arriving, as well as while traveling. This decision will be aided by MSFS 2024's real-time weather data.
- ✦ **Getting Ready for Takeoff:** Aircraft Configuration: Make sure your aircraft is set up for IFR flying before you leave.
  - ➢ **Avionics:** Configure VORs and ILS frequencies on your navigation radios.
  - ➢ **Autopilot:** Select the navigation, heading, and altitude hold modes.
  - ➢ **Flight Instruments:** Verify that every flight instrument is functional and configured for the appropriate units.
  - ➢ **Procedures and Charts:** Learn about and get acquainted with the necessary IFR charts. This should have DP, en route charts, and STARs, among other things. MSFS 2024 makes a large range of charts available.
- ✦ **Procedures for Departure**
  - ➢ **ATIS Information:** To get the most recent weather and airport information, first listen into the Automatic Terminal Information Service (ATIS) frequency.
  - ➢ **Clearance Delivery:** Get IFR clearance for your route, starting altitude, and squawk code by calling ATC.
  - ➢ **Taxi and Takeoff:** Follow ATC's instructions for taxiing and taking off. Pay attention to the circumstances, particularly when visibility is limited.
- ✦ **Operations While Traveling**
  - ➢ **Navigation:** Systems that make it possible to follow the intended path. To assist in this process, MSFS 2024 includes navigation aids that are reasonably realistic.
  - ➢ **Altitude Management:** Observe designated heights and anticipate altitude variations as directed by ATC.
  - ➢ **Communication:** Stay in touch with ATC about things like location and altitude. Regarding departure from the flying plan as well.
- ✦ **Approach and Arrival**
  - ➢ **Arrival protocols:** Follow all approach charts and arrival protocols to reach the destination. These graphics are part of MSFS 2024 to help in decision-making.
  - ➢ **Approach Clearance:** Obtain ATC's approval for the approach process.
  - ➢ **Approach Execution:** Use navigational aids and instruments to navigate to the runway while you carry out the approach process.
- ✦ **Arrival and After Takeoff**
  - ➢ **Landing:** Use the proper speeds and configuration to land the aircraft in accordance with the approach method.

- ➢ **Cab and Shutdown:** As directed by ATC, take a cab to the gate or parking area after landing. To secure the aircraft, according to the post-flight checklist.

Performing Navigation under Visual Flight Rules (VFR)

The method of flying an airplane using visual references on the ground, known as Visual Flight Rules (VFR) navigation, enables the pilot to maintain situational awareness of other aircraft and objects in order to navigate safely. This is the foundation of all VFR flying and works best in favorable weather.

Organizing Your VFR Flight

- ✦ **Path Selection:** Make sure your path follows well-known landmarks like roads, rivers, and unique topography. This method improves situational awareness and facilitates navigation.
- ✦ **Weather Check:** Verify that the present weather is under VFR conditions before leaving. Because MSFS 2024 provides real-time weather information, precise planning is possible.
- ✦ **Flight Planning Features:** MSFS 2024 has integrated flight planning features. These tools allow waypoint selection and provide a detailed plotted route, both of which are helpful for route visualization.

Navigation using VFR in MSFS 2024

- ✦ **Getting Ready for Flight:**
  - ➢ **Aircraft Preparation:** Configure the navigation systems of your aircraft, making sure that all of the instruments are calibrated and operational.
  - ➢ **Charts and Briefing:** Review the VFR charts that apply to your route and provide a comprehensive pre-flight briefing on probable hazards and landmarks
- ✦ **Departing:**
  - ➢ **Visual References:** To ascertain your location right after takeoff, locate notable landmarks and align yourself with them.
  - ➢ **Altitude management:** Stay at a height that allows for safe maneuvering and unobstructed views of the terrain.
- ✦ **Navigation While En Route:**
  - ➢ **Landmark Identification:** To confirm location, constantly search for and validate landmarks. Keeping situational awareness is essential.

- ➤ **Course Modifications:** Be ready for any required course modifications, particularly in the event of unforeseen weather or airspace constraints.
- ♦ **Landing and Approach:**
  - ➤ **Visual Approach:** Taking wind conditions into account, visually plan your approach to line up with the runways.
  - ➤ **Landing routine:** Make sure the runway and the surrounding landscape are visible by following the landing routine.

Utilizing the Features of MSFS 2024 for VFR Navigation

A number of improvements in MSFS 2024 improve VFR navigation, such as:
- ♦ **Realistic landscape Rendering:** The simulator's sophisticated visuals provide landscape and landmark representations authenticity, enabling visual navigation in the event of an accident.
- ♦ **Dynamic Weather System:** Accurate flight planning and in-flight route modifications to avoid inclement weather are made possible by real-time weather updates.
- ♦ **Integrated Flight Planning:** Pilots may use this simulator's flight-planning capabilities to map out a route, choose waypoints, and chart courses in the most efficient manner.

Useful Advice

- ♦ **Start Easy:** Before trying longer flights, begin with short, local flights to get acquainted with VFR navigation techniques.
- ♦ **Use VFR Charts:** To improve realism and comprehend navigation concepts, use real-world VFR charts in your preparation.
- ♦ **Practice Often:** The secret to being proficient in VFR navigation is regular practice. Frequent flying will gradually boost your confidence and ability level.

Managing Emergency Protocols

MSFS 2024's emergency procedures are based on actual aviation standards, providing the most realistic virtual learning environment. The simulator has checklists and scenarios that are sufficiently realistic to simulate a variety of crises, including bad weather, electrical failure, and engine failure. A pilot may respond appropriately in emergency circumstances by being aware of these protocols.

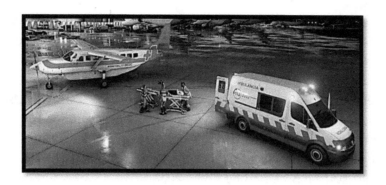

Making Use of In-Game Resources

MSFS 2024 has a number of features to assist a pilot in handling emergencies:

- **Checklists:** The pilot will be directed through both routine and emergency procedures using checklists that are guided by an integrated checklist system. Every checklist is completely customizable and accessible from the game's interface. The SDK documentation, for example, outlines the recommended practices for developing and using checklists. By doing this, they will be guaranteed to adhere to the broad criteria that the airplanes in the simulator utilize.

- **Cockpit Interaction System:** Pilots may engage with aircraft controls and systems in real time using MSFS 2024's cockpit interaction system. When the pilot has to take certain measures, like shutting down the engine or deploying emergency equipment, this is crucial.

- **Training Missions:** This simulator's training missions may also mimic crises and provide practical experience in a safe, non-threatening setting. Gaining a great deal of confidence in managing serious crises requires this kind of training.

Top Techniques for Managing Emergencies

- **Getting Ready and Acquainted:**
  - **Study of Aircraft Systems:** It is essential to be familiar with the particular systems and constraints of the aircraft being flown. Every aircraft in MSFS 2024 is different, having special traits and protocols for handling emergencies. For instance, the MSFS forums include a fairly thorough flight manual for the Heart Aerospace ES-30 that covers system administration, starting procedures, and flying phases.
  - **Examine the following emergency checklists:** Being prepared is aided by the practice and regular review of emergency checklists. There are

instructions on how to make efficient checklists in the SDK documentation. It views text, assessment, and visual assistance as the most important.

- **In the event of an emergency:**
  - ➢ **Remain Calm, Assess the Situation:** Make a decision right away regarding the emergency's nature and the state of the aircraft. Use the cockpit interaction system to keep an eye on the systems and instruments.
  - ➢ **Adhere to established protocols:** Observe the relevant emergency checklist. You can follow the steps in a methodical and efficient manner by using the checklist system provided by MSFS 2024.
  - ➢ **Communicate with ATC:** To notify air traffic control of the emergency, use the in-game ATC system to call them. Coordinating help and guaranteeing safety depend heavily on communication.
- **Actions Taken After an Emergency:**
  - ➢ **Perform a Comprehensive Debriefing:** After handling the emergency, conduct a thorough debriefing, examining what was done and identifying areas for improvement. You can get useful information and comments by participating in discussions in the MSFS community forums.
  - ➢ **Practice Often:** Practicing emergency situations on a regular basis improves confidence and skill. Practice different MSFS 2024 training missions and independently develop some unique emergency scenarios.

Practice Advanced Maneuvers

In order to overcome various flight situations, pilots employ a variety of extremely complex techniques known as advanced flight maneuvers. Such maneuvers are crucial for gaining situational awareness, making sound decisions, and becoming proficient in aircraft control. **Here are a few typical advanced maneuvers:**

- **Stall Recovery:** For low speed safety, this is a crucial recovery technique to perfect.
- **Spin Avoidance and Recovery:** For pilot safety, one has to understand how to prevent spins and how to recover from them.
- **Crosswind Landings:** Managing meteorological circumstances requires the skill to land in crosswinds.
- **Instrument Approaches:** Approaching solely with instrument references is basic for the instrument-rated pilot.

Practice Advanced Maneuvers

For practicing these maneuvers in flight, MSFS 2024 provides realistic flying experience.

Here is how you can effectively practice with the simulator:

- **Select the Correct Aircraft:** You will pick a suitable aircraft that will enable you to practice the kind of maneuver you are interested in. For instance, the Cessna 172 applies to learning stalls or crosswind landing.
- **Create a Realistic Situation:** To make your sessions as realistic as possible, make sure it replicates circumstances from real life, including the time of day, the weather, and even traffic.
- **Use Training Modules:** MSFS 2024 has built-in modules that will walk you through different maneuvers. To help you improve in each training area, the training modules come with comprehensive instructions and tests.
- **Include Third-Party Add-Ons:** Third-party add-ons that provide sophisticated training situations with very thorough lessons can be necessary for further specialized training.

Advantages of Using Advanced Maneuvers

A few of the main benefits of performing advanced maneuvers in MSFS 2024 are as follows:

- **Safety:** Practice complex scenarios, not taking into consideration any risks associated with training in the real world.
- **Economical:** Using a flight simulator eliminates the need to pay instructors, rent an aircraft, or buy fuel.
- **Flexibility:** Training sessions may be scheduled around your availability, you can repeat moves as required, and you can practice at your own speed.
- **Instant Feedback:** The majority of simulators provide instant feedback about your performance, allowing you to identify areas for improvement.

Understanding Aerodynamics and Flight Physics

Aerodynamics is the study of the interaction between air and objects in motion. It plays a very crucial function in flight simulation. MSFS 2024 incorporates a new physics engine, allowing the simulation of more than 10,000 rigid-body surfaces and properly simulating varied aircraft forms and behaviors. This enables for improved modeling of lift, drag, and other aerodynamic forces, allowing users to better mimic flight. The soft body physics of the simulator further increases the realism via the modeling of materials like fabric, ropes, and balloons. This is best illustrated in the modeling of hot air balloons, wherein the dynamics of inflation, deflation, and flight are reproduced with amazing realism.

High-Tech Avionics and Aircraft Systems

MSFS 2024 offers additional realism to aircraft systems, such as electrical, pneumatic, fuel, and hydraulic. Furthermore, the simulation is further enhanced by the inclusion of avionics such the Honeywell Primus Epic 2 and Universal UNS-1 FMS. Preflight inspections and walkaround checks are offered for the pilots to immerse them more into flight.

Flight Planning and Navigation

The simulator contains an integrated and revolutionary flight planner capable of handling both IFR and VFR flying. Fully featured comprehensive charts, route planning, fuel and cargo computation, vertical profile planning, and ETOPS planning. Moreover, pertinent airport information is accessible, such as weather and NOTAMs, inside the simulator or on mobile devices and online browsers.

Simulating the Weather and Landscape

The 2024 version unveils an astonishing visual with Earth's digital twin, exhibiting superior digital elevation maps, more than 500 TIN cities, and over 100,000 square kilometers of photogrammetry. All 40,000 airports, 80,000 helipads, 1.5 billion buildings, and over 3 trillion trees are dynamically created in situ by its procedural algorithm. The environment is illuminated more precisely than before thanks to the photometric lighting system, and improved weather characteristics like auroras and new kinds of clouds provide an engrossing atmospheric experience.

Flight Dynamics That Are Realistic

This is made feasible by MSFS 2024's new physics engine, which allows for very precise simulation of a variety of aerodynamic factors, including drag, turbulence, and lift force. Pilots would be able to experience the nuances of flying in various aircraft under various situations as a result.

CHAPTER FIFTEEN

INTEGRATION OF VIRTUAL REALITY (VR)

Configuring VR Hardware

For optimal performance and quality, setting up VR gear requires extensive planning. **Here is a thorough tutorial to help you navigate it:**

- **Selecting the Proper VR Headset:** Choosing a VR headset that works with your system and MSFS 2024 should be your first priority. **Several well-liked options are:**
  - **Oculus Quest 2/3:** This gadget may be used alone, but for better performance, it can also be connected to a PC.
  - The high-resolution HP Reverb G2 monitor is perfect for detailed cockpit views.
  - **Valve Index:** High refresh rates and a broad field of vision significantly improve immersion.
  - Make that the GPU, CPU, and USB ports on your PC meet the minimal requirements for headsets.
  - **Getting Your Computer Ready:** For a VR experience to work well, a strong PC setup is required. **The primary factors to be taken into account are:**
  - **Graphics Card (GPU):** For the detailed depiction of surroundings, a strong GPU from a series like NVIDIA RTX is essential.
  - **CPU:** Given the effectiveness of data processing, it should have a multi-core CPU, such the AMD Ryzen or Intel i7/i9 series.
  - **Memory (RAM):** To handle VR-based applications, a minimum of 16GB of RAM is advised.
  - **USB Ports:** Enough USB ports are required to connect headphones and other accessories.
  - For optimum performance, you must update your system drivers on a regular basis, particularly the GPU drivers.
- **Setting Up VR Software:** Proprietary software is included with every VR headset to make connecting and setup easier:
  - **Oculus:** Set up the Oculus app on your computer by following the setup guidelines.
  - **HP Reverb G2:** To configure, use the Windows Mixed Reality site.
  - **Valve Index:** For calibration and setting, use SteamVR.
  - These apps will walk you through the calibration and installation procedures so your headset is operational.

- **Setting up MSFS 2024 for Virtual Reality:** After your VR gear is operational, configure MSFS 2024 for optimal performance:
  - **MSFS 2024 Launch:** Turn on the simulator on your screen.
  - **Turning on VR Mode:** To enter VR mode, press Ctrl + Tab. To prevent problems, make sure the simulator is operating in full-screen mode.
  - **Modify VR Settings:** To modify more complex settings like resolution, field of vision, and comfort settings, choose Options > General > Graphics > VR.
  - Try adjusting these parameters to strike a balance between performance and visual quality.
- **Enhancing Efficiency:** Optimization is necessary for seamless VR performance:
  - **Graphics Settings:** You may increase frame rates by lowering settings like anti-aliasing and shadow quality.
  - **Resolution Scaling:** You may improve clarity without taxing the GPU too much by adjusting the render scale.
  - **Third-Party Tools:** OpenXR Toolkit facilitates the modification of parameters like field of vision and motion reprojection.
  - To guarantee smoothness, performance measurements should be examined on a frequent basis.
- **Improving the Experience:** Enhancing your virtual reality experience even more:
  - **Control Setup:** Set up your yoke or joystick to control VR features, such switching between VR modes.
  - **Comfort Settings:** To lessen motion sickness, change comfort settings like vignette effects and snap-turning.
  - **Peripheral Integration:** To enhance simulation realism, include additional peripherals such as throttle quadrants and rudder pedals.
- **Solving Typical Problems:** Be ready for the following potential issues:
  - **Performance Drops:** You may increase frame rates by lowering some graphical settings or modifying resolution scaling.
  - **Motion Sickness:** To assist reduce discomfort, adjust comfort settings and take regular rests.
  - **Connectivity Problems:** Verify that your PC recognizes the VR headset and that all wires are plugged in correctly.

The issue is frequently resolved by looking for specific solutions in community forums and official support channels.

Setting Up VR Preferences in the Simulator

The secret to having excellent performance and graphics in virtual reality is to properly configure the settings. **This detailed guide will assist you in configuring virtual reality in MSFS 2024.**

- **System prerequisites:** Verify that their system can manage VR settings before delving further into them:
  - ➤ **OS:** at least Windows 10.
  - ➤ **Processor:** AMD Ryzen 5 1500X or Intel Core i5-8400.
  - ➤ 16 GB of RAM for memory.
  - ➤ **Graphics card:** AMD Radeon RX 5700 or NVIDIA GeForce GTX 1080.
  - ➤ **Headset VR:** To work with the VR headset of your choice.
- **Configuring Your Virtual Reality Headset**
  - ➤ **Installation:** Assist the manufacturer in installing your VR headset.
  - ➤ **Software Installation:** Set up the necessary software, which includes SteamVR for the HTC Vive and the Oculus app for Oculus headsets.
  - ➤ **Calibration:** Adjust the headset's settings to guarantee precise tracking and comfort.
- **Setting up virtual reality in MSFS 2024**
  - ➤ **Starting VR Mode:**
    - ✓ To switch to VR mode, use Ctrl + Tab.
    - ✓ As an alternative, choose the VR option from the in-game menu.
  - ➤ **VR in-game settings:**
    - ✓ Select General > VR under Options.

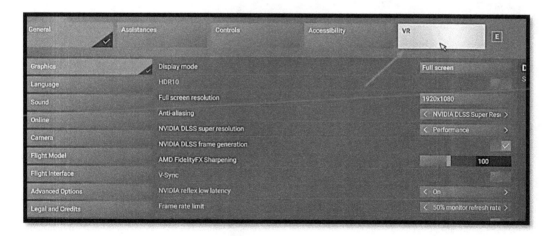

- ✓ **Render scaling:** Modify to strike a balance between visual quality and performance.

- ✓ **Anti-aliasing:** DLSS Quality is selected for better graphics with little effect on performance.
- ✓ For more intricate texturing, use a high texture resolution.
- ✓ **Shadow Maps:** Excellent for depicting really lifelike shadows.
- ✓ **Terrain Shadows:** Elevated for fine ground details.
- ✓ **Contact shadows:** For realistic contact shadows, set the value high.
- ✓ **Windshield effects:** High for effects that are realistic.
- ✓ For realistic light effects, use high light shafts.
- ✓ **Brightness:** High: More lifelike lighting effects.
- ✓ **Lens Flare:** High: Lens flares effects that are more lifelike.
- ✓ **Light Scattering:** High: Light scattering effects that are more realistic.
- ✓ **Ambient Occlusion:** High: More accurate effects of ambient occlusion.
- ✓ **Reflections:** High: Reflections that is more accurate.
- ✓ **Refraction:** High: Refraction effects are more realistic.
- ✓ **High-Realistic Cloud Rendering:** Volumetric Clouds.
- ✓ Performance is enhanced by turning off texture super sampling.
- ✓ **Motion Reprojection:** To reduce latency, this should be disabled.
- ✓ **World Scale:** Modify this to match your actual environment.
- ✓ **VR Cockpit Interaction System:** To use conventional controls, switch this to Legacy.
- ✓ **VR Controller Interaction System:** To utilize conventional controls, switch this to Legacy.

⬥ **Enhancing Efficiency**
- ➤ **Frame Rate Limiting:** For more fluid gaming, it is advised to lock the frame rate at 45 FPS. Smooth performance and quality are provided by this kind of balancing, particularly in scenarios that are dramatic.

- ➢ Use Deep Learning Super Sampling (DLSS) to get the greatest images at the lowest possible performance costs. With little frame rate loss, DLSS in Quality mode significantly improves picture quality.
- ➢ **SteamVR Settings:** For those who use SteamVR, the following option is a suitable one to utilize:
  - ✓ **Motion Smoothing:** Turn off to cut down on latency.
  - ✓ For clarity, use a custom resolution multiplier of 140%.
  - ✓ For natural viewing, the field of vision is 100%.
  - ✓ To ensure precise scale, turn off the world scale.
  - ✓ For the least amount of lag, turn off the legacy projection mode.
  - ✓ **Throttling Behavior:** Adjusted for reliable operation.
  - ✓ For more fluid performance, set the lock app framerate to 45 frames per second.
  - ✓ Extra Forecast: 0.00 to reduce latency.

These will contribute to VR's increased clarity and fluidity.

- ✦ **VR Cockpit Interaction**
  - ➢ Using VR controls to navigate the cockpit may be rather novel. Users can interact with buttons, switches, and dials much more intuitively because to MSFS 2024's VR-specific interaction technologies. To improve accuracy and responsiveness for these kinds of interactions, you may need to adjust your settings.
  - ➢ **VR Cockpit Interaction System:** Choose the most comfortable interaction system from the VR settings. There are often two options: "Legacy" and "Interaction." Some users like the Legacy system since it functions similarly to the outdated mouse-based interaction while still providing a great deal of tactile VR experience. The more sophisticated interaction system, which will enable precise VR controller inputs to interact with different cockpit aspects, could be more appealing to others.
  - ➢ **Mouse or VR Controllers:** For cockpit interactions in virtual reality, you have the option of using a mouse or VR controllers. By just staring at the cockpit interface with your head and using the mouse to click on different switches, you may use the mouse even in VR mode if you prefer more conventional mouse controls. Though it could take some getting accustomed to the button layouts and the distance between each control, VR controllers provide a more engaging interaction experience.
- ✦ **Adjustments for the VR Controller and Headset**
  - ➢ **Flying in VR:** Adjusting the headset and controller positions is crucial for comfort and immersion. To prevent blur, adjust the VR headset's straps so

that the lenses are the ideal distance from your eyes. In order to view the cockpit clearly and without strain, adjust the focus distance to fit your eyes.

- ➢ **Controller Position:** Having your VR controllers properly adjusted to match your actual area is a smart idea. You may adjust the positional offset of the controller in MSFS 2024. Ensure that controls are conveniently accessible and at arm's length. Try out different controller configurations and mappings until you're at ease.
- ➢ **Headset Fitting:** The headset's fit is equally crucial. Your eyes may strain or become uncomfortable if your headset is too tight or too loose. Additionally, confirm that the lens spacing is adjusted appropriately for your eyes. Immersion may be hampered by visual discomfort caused by too wide or narrow lens spacing.

Improvements to Immersion

- ➢ For a more immersive VR experience, additional hardware integrations like motion platforms, haptic feedback devices, or other accessories like yokes and throttle quadrants would be a smart choice. With the pressures and vibrations that one would experience during a genuine flight, these gadgets may further enhance the VR experience's sense of realism. Make sure, nevertheless, that the hardware of your machine can handle them without experiencing any performance issues.
- ➢ **Motion Platforms:** Motion platforms, such as those from SimXperience or Next Level Racing, may simulate the forces of banking, braking, and acceleration for players seeking a greater degree of realism. These platforms may elevate your experience, but they are pricey.
- ➢ **Haptic Feedback:** You may experience the unconventional reaction of the aircraft controls with the Honeycomb Bravo Throttle Quadrant or Thrustmaster TCA Officer Pack's realistic flight haptic feedback. When using the throttle, speed brakes, or rudder, this kind of input will be most useful.

Using VR to Navigate the Cockpit

Navigating the Cockpit in virtual reality is an intriguing and distinct task that calls for both technical setup and adjustment to new interface techniques.

Configuring VR in MSFS 2024

Make sure your VR equipment is configured properly before beginning to learn how to navigate the cockpit. Oculus, HTC Vive, and Valve Index are VR headsets that MSFS 2024 natively supports.

To get things started:
- **Install Required Software:** Get and set up the most recent VR headset drivers and software.
- **To set up MSFS 2024**, go to the settings menu in the simulator and choose VR. To fit your tastes, change factors like resolution, field of view, and comfort settings.
- **Adjust Controls:** Verify that your VR controllers or any appropriate accessories are mapped and operating properly.

Using VR to Navigate the Cockpit

Interacting with the cockpit becomes haptic after VR is configured. Here are some important factors to think about:
- **Cockpit Communication:**
  - **Touch Controls:** The majority of MSFS 2024 aircraft include touch controls, which let users interface with the different cockpit components directly. Touch levers, knobs, and switches using your fingers. For instance, you can reach in and adjust the mixture and throttle controls on a Cessna 172.
  - **VR Controllers:** Use your controllers to interact with cockpit features if your aircraft allows VR controller interaction. Make that the simulator recognizes and configures your controllers correctly.
- **Readability of Instruments:**
  - **Clarity Adjustment:** It might sometimes be difficult to read the instruments in virtual reality. Navigate to the simulator's settings and change the text's contrast and size. It is advised to experiment with these settings since there have been some complaints of problems with instrument clarity in MSFS 2024.
  - **Head Positioning:** To observe the instruments, adjust your head accordingly. You may zoom in on certain panels or adjust your seat position in some planes.
- **Navigating the Menu:**
  - **In-Flight Menus:** Using virtual reality to view in-flight menus might be challenging. According to certain accounts, MSFS 2024 menu navigation may be challenging. To access menus, use voice commands or designate certain buttons on your VR controllers.
  - **External Tools:** To manage flight plans and settings and eliminate the need to explore in-game menus, it is a good idea to utilize external tools like tablets or cellphones.
- **Safety and Comfort:**

- ➢ **Modify Settings:** Use the comfort settings for vignette effects and motion smoothing to prevent VR weariness. To make flying in virtual reality more enjoyable, MSFS 2024 offers a number of comfort choices.
- ➢ **Take rests:** To prevent any pain and preserve the feeling of immersion, take frequent rests.

Obstacles and Things to Think About

Even though MSFS 2024's VR is quite immersive, there are a number of issues:
- ✦ **Performance Problems:** A few users have complained about graphical flaws and frame rate decreases while using VR mode. Make sure your system satisfies the suggested requirements, and for best results, think about modifying the graphics settings.
- ✦ **Controller Compatibility:** VR controller interaction is not supported by every plane. For instance, certain aircraft may not have VR-compatible throttles or yokes. Prior to trying VR interactions, make sure the aircraft is compatible.
- ✦ **Learning Curve:** Getting used to VR takes time. Spend some time acclimating to the immersive world and familiarizing yourself with the new interaction techniques.

Resolving VR Problems

This section provides a list of troubleshooting techniques for typical VR problems with MSFS 2024.
- ✦ **Errors in Initialization**
  - ➢ **Issue:** When you start MSFS 2024, you get an error message stating, "The initialization of VR failed."
  - ➢ **Fix:** Configure the OpenXR Runtime:
    - ✓ Launch SteamVR.
    - ✓ Select Show under Advanced Settings > Developer under Settings.
    - ✓ Click on Current OpenXR Runtime and choose "OpenXR runtime."
    - ✓ Try launching MSFS 2024 again and navigating to VR mode.
- ✦ **VR Black Screen**
  - ➢ **Issue:** The screen becomes dark when VR is enabled.
  - ➢ **Fix: Turn off HDR:**
    - ✓ In Windows, choose Display under Settings > System.
    - ✓ Toggle HDR off in the Advanced Display options.
    - ✓ Disable HDR in MSFS 2024 by going to Options > General > Graphics.
- ✦ **Deterioration of Performance**
  - ➢ **Issue:** Compared to earlier iterations, VR performance is worse.
  - ➢ **Fixes:**

- ✓ **Adjust Graphics Settings:** Disable Render Scaling, Terrain Level of Detail and Object Level of Detail.
- ✓ **Update Drivers:** Maintain the most recent GPU drivers.
- ✓ **Close Background Applications:** Clear off unnecessary and superfluous apps to free up system resources.

Virtual Reality Black Box

- ➤ **Problem:** When you go to Virtual Reality Mode, a big black box appears in front of you.
- ➤ **Fixes:** Oculus software update:
  - ✓ Verify that the most recent version of the Oculus software is installed.
- ➤ **Modify the settings for the Oculus Debug Tool:**
  - ✓ Find Oculus Debug, which is often located in C:\\Program Files\\Oculus\\Support\\oculus-diagnostics.
  - ✓ Open Use FOV Stencil and change its option to Off.
  - ✓ Restart MSFS 2024 after that to see whether the issue still exists.

Mouse and Toolbar Problems

- ➤ **Issue:** The mouse is sluggish in VR and the toolbar isn't loading correctly.
- ➤ **Fixes:**
  - ✓ **Reset Controls:** In MSFS 2024, choose Options > Controls and return to the original configuration.
  - ✓ **Adjust Mouse Settings:** To adjust the mouse settings for VR in MSFS 2024, choose Options > General > Accessibility.

Problems with Exposure and Lighting

- ➤ **Issue:** When utilizing VR, overexposure and detail loss occur in bright regions.
- ➤ **Fixes:**
  - ✓ **Modify In-Sim Preferences:** In MSFS 2024, choose Options > General > Graphics and modify the Gamma, Contrast, and Brightness parameters.
  - ✓ **Disable Eye Adaptation:** According to some users, this might be beneficial.

Problems with Sound

- ➤ **Issue:** VR flights don't have sound.
- ➤ **Fixes:**
  - ✓ **Verify Audio Settings:** Make sure that Windows and MSFS 2024 are using the correct audio output device.
  - ✓ **Update Audio Drivers:** Verify that the audio drivers on your computer have been updated.

Accidents in Virtual Reality

- ➤ **Issue:** When MSFS 2024 tries to enter VR mode, it crashes.
- ➤ **Fix:** Turn off the desktop theater mode for SteamVR:

- ✓ Launch Steam.
- ✓ Select Steam > In-Game > Settings.
- ✓ When SteamVR is running, uncheck the box for "Use Desktop Theater."
- ✓ Try to access VR mode after restarting MSFS 2024.
- ⬥ **Compatibility of ReShade**
  - ➤ **Issue:** ReShade's VR mode isn't functioning correctly.
  - ➤ **Fix:** Install ReShade with OpenXR and DX12; under the rendering API choice, make sure that OpenXR and DX12 are chosen. Additionally, to access the ReShade menu in VR, use the Home key.

Improving the Performance of VR

In order to provide high-quality images at high frame rates for an uncomfortable experience, virtual reality applications need a significant amount of processing power. The extensive surroundings and sophisticated visuals in MSFS 2024 might strain technology, leading to stuttering, poor frame rates, and even motion sickness.

Optimization of in-game settings

To strike a balance between performance and graphic quality, several in-game adjustments need be made. It is advised to use the following settings:
- ⬥ Render scaling: Start at 80% and go up for better graphics if performance permits.
- ⬥ **Anti-aliasing:** For smooth edges, use TAA.
- ⬥ 'Depth' is the setting for the projection mode to improve frame time.
- ⬥ **Anisotropic Filtering:** 16x for textures that are clear; lower if performance problems arise.
- ⬥ **Global Render Quality:** A decent place to start is with Medium.
- ⬥ To balance performance and intricacy, the Terrain Level of intricacy (LoD) is set at 85%.
- ⬥ To increase responsiveness, the cockpit refresh rate is kept low.
- ⬥ **Visual Effects:** You should disable the resource-intensive elements, such as Bloom, Depth of Field, Lens Correction, and Lens Flare.
- ⬥ **Clouds and Shadows:** The GPU burden should be reduced by turning off Terrain Shadows and using Volumetric Clouds Low.
- ⬥ **Texture Settings:** 4x4 Texture Supersampling and Medium Resolution provide a compromise between performance and quality.

By making these changes, VR performance will be more fluid without significantly compromising visual quality.

Hardware Points to Remember

The way MSFS 2024 runs in virtual reality is mostly dependent on your hardware setup. When combined with powerful CPUs and plenty of RAM, high-end GPUs like the NVIDIA RTX 4090 or RTX 4080 may push settings higher, but mid-range systems must be more cautious for seamless performance.

Making Use of Advanced Features

A number of cutting-edge features that MSFS 2024 enables may enhance VR performance:

- **Focused Rendering:** By lowering the resolution at the edges of the field of view, this technique lowers the rendering demand. When used properly, foveated rendering may greatly improve speed without sacrificing visual quality.
- **Deep Learning Super Sampling (DLSS):** DLSS use artificial intelligence (AI) to upscale pictures with lower resolutions to much higher resolutions for greater frame rates with little visual quality loss. DLSS in 'Quality' mode could provide a decent balance between picture quality and performance.

Optimizations at the System Level

System-level tweaks may enhance VR performance even more than in-game settings:

- **Update Drivers:** For the newest bug fixes and performance improvements, make sure the drivers for your VR headset and GPU are up to date.
- **Close Background Apps:** To save system resources, close any unused programs.
- The power plan on your PC should be set to 'High Performance' in order to prevent throttling.
- **Make Use of Dedicated Storage:** To speed up loading times and improve overall performance, MSFS 2024 should be set up on a dedicated SSD.

CHAPTER SIXTEEN
USING CO-PILOT FEATURES AND CHECKLISTS
Checklists for In-Game Access

Checklists are included into the Electronic Flight Bag (EFB) in MSFS 2024, offering a thorough and engaging experience.

To get the checklists:
- The EFB may be accessed by pressing the 'TAB' default key. The checklist is one of the many tools and information available on this interface.
- **Access the Checklist Section:** Find and choose the 'Checklist' tab in the EFB. A list of available checklists customized for your aircraft may be found in this section.
- **Pick a List of Items:** Choose the relevant checklist, which may be either Before Taxi or Pre-flight. Next, page after page of a chosen checklist's processes are shown, with many checkpoints on each page.
- **Examine and record checkpoints:** By checking off items on a checklist, you can be sure that everything is done.

It should be noted that MSFS 2024 calls up the checklist nearly entirely via the EFB rather than a UI panel, in contrast to MSFS 2020. The checklist's deeper integration with the aircraft's systems tends to improve the user experience.

Making Use of Co-Pilot Features

For many flying tasks, MSFS 2024 offers co-pilot capabilities to increase realism and provide support during intricate operations.

To get access to:

- **Go to Co-Pilot Settings:** Launch the EFB and choose the 'Co-Pilot' or 'Assisted Checklist' area to control the settings for this.
- **Adjust help Level:** Depending on your comfort level and flying expertise, you must adjust the settings to determine how much Full, Assisted, or Manual co-pilot help it will provide.
- **Turn on Co-Pilot Assistance:** Following setup, co-pilot assistance has to be turned on. While you do other flight-related tasks, the co-pilot may operate the autopilot, progress checklists, and communicate via radios.

Comprehending Co-Pilot Support

Co-Pilot Assistance in MSFS 2024 is intended to assist pilots by taking over some duties automatically, freeing them up to concentrate more on crucial flight operations. **This system has a number of important features:**

- **Automated Checklist Management:** By lessening the cognitive strain on the captain, the co-pilot will automate checklists for the completion of all pre-, in-, and post-flight procedures, increasing procedural correctness.
- **Communication Handling:** Radio broadcasts and answers are among the communications that the co-pilot manages with air traffic control. In this sense, it streamlines the communication process and keeps the pilot out of such crucial situations.
- **Flight Path Assistance:** In order to keep the aircraft on track, the co-pilot may help manage its flight path by adjusting the autopilot and making navigational adjustments.

Utilizing the Features for Co-Pilot Assistance

Use the following procedures to use MSFS 2024's Co-Pilot Assistance features:

- **Co-Pilot Settings Opening:** Select 'Assistance' from the simulator's menu. Click on the 'Co-Pilot' tab in the menu that appears to see a variety of help alternatives.
- **Establishing Assistance Levels:** Modify the assistance levels for various tasks including communication and checklists. Choose between total automation and fully manual control based on your skills and preferences.
- **Facilitating Co-Pilot Functionalities:** Activate certain Co-Pilot functions that are required while in flight, such checklist management and ATC communication.

While in flight, keep an eye on the co-pilot's operations to make sure things are being handled the way you want them to.

Limitations and Considerations

Despite its greatness, MSFS 2024's Co-Pilot Assistance technology has many drawbacks. They are:
+ **Feature Availability:** MSFS 2024 may not include all of the functions that were available in previous iterations, such as Co-Pilot reading and checklist management. In fact, customers have complained that this function, which was one of MSFS 2020's highlights, has been removed.
+ **Limited Customization:** Compared to earlier iterations, the degree of customization available for Co-Pilot assistance may be relatively limited, which might impact the system's capacity to be tailored to individual tastes.
+ **Performance Could Change:** The aircraft model and particular flight circumstances will determine how effectively the Co-Pilot features function. In fact, customers have complained about the Co-Pilot's uneven performance in various scenarios.

Automating Typical Processes

Automated Checklists

Checklists are immediately included into the Electronic Flight Bag in MSFS 2024, accessible via the in-game tablet. To access the tablet, use the TAB key, click the airplane symbol, and choose "Checklist." The pilot may simply alter and adhere to a checklist using this interface. The virtual co-pilot may carry out checklist items automatically thanks to the copilot action's auto-complete capability. For those who want to automate routine processes so that important activities are carried out without their involvement, this function is helpful.

How to Activate the Helped Checklist

To activate Assisted Checklist in MSFS 2024, go to the in-game menu options and do the following:
+ When the in-game menu appears, choose "Options."
+ Select "Assistance" from the menu.
+ Make sure the "Assisted Checklist" option is set to "On."

With this configuration, the virtual co-pilot may help with checklists during supported tasks and free flight. Turning on this feature increases the automation of common tasks inside the checklist interface and opens up more possibilities.

Adapting Checklists to Various Aircraft

In MSFS 2024, checklists are essential to flight safety and efficiency since they guide users through the steps to do before, during, and after a flight. It does provide a useful structure for developing and modifying checklists for different kinds of aircraft.

Getting to Know and Changing Checklists

Here's a detailed guide on how to access and modify checklists in MSFS 2024:
- **Launch the In-Sim Toolbar:** To launch the in-sim toolbar in MSFS, hit the TAB key.
- **Select the airplane Icon:** Select the toolbar's airplane icon.
- **Choose Checklist:** This brings up a drop-down menu with every checklist for your current aircraft that is accessible.
- **Edit Checklist:** You may add, delete, or modify items from your checklist using the choices on the checklist interface.

Pilots may then modify checklists to fit their jobs or even specific aircraft configurations.

The Best Methods for Customizing Checklists

The following are some recommended practices to consider while modifying checklists for uniformity and security:
- **Normal Procedures:** Verify that the checklist's items adhere to the aircraft model's normal operating procedures.
- **Preserve Logical Flow:** Arrange the checklist items from pre-flight to shut-down in a logical order that corresponds to the flying phases.
- **Frequent Update:** Examine checklists often to account for any modifications brought about by upgrades to aircraft configuration or adjustments to procedures.

Pilots may develop checklists that will successfully enhance flying performance and safety by adhering to these guidelines.

Co-Pilot Capabilities for MSFS 2024

With MSFS 2024, co-pilot functionality becomes more realistic. The virtual copilot may be tasked with a few duties. **However, take note that the copilot's skills have evolved:**
- **ATC Communication:** The co-pilot is capable of managing radio communications, handling air traffic control communications, and making sure that ATC directives are followed.

- **Flight Control:** In MSFS 2024, the co-pilot is unable to operate the aircraft or oversee checklists, in contrast to earlier iterations. Users who miss the co-pilot's ability to read and auto-complete checklists have pointed out this issue.

Controlling Co-Pilot Characteristics

To control MSFS 2024's co-pilot features:
- To access Assistance Settings, go to the simulator's 'Assistance' menu.
- **Adjust Realism Settings:** Go to the bottom of the 'Realism' page, where 'AI Radio' is situated.
- **Activate/Disable Co-Pilot:** To activate or disable the co-pilot, tick the box next to it.

Pilots may use this parameter to gauge how much the co-pilot is helping them with flying responsibilities.

Using Co-Pilot Features to Improve Workflow

The Co-Pilot function has been redesigned for MSFS 2024 to be much more helpful and communicative during flight operations. The new simulator's Co-Pilot, in contrast to its predecessor, provides visual signals and assistance via the Electronic Flight Bag (EFB), which is connected with the aircraft's equipment. This makes the simulation's atmosphere much more realistic and coherent.

Using Co-Pilot Features to Improve Workflow

- **Assisted Checklists:** To make sure that the crucial tasks are completed in the correct order, the Co-Pilot may assist in overseeing the checklists. This feature is highly helpful for complex operations and reduces the pilot's effort by reducing the likelihood of missing crucial stages. However, compared to earlier versions, several users have noted that MSFS 2024's Co-Pilot's capacity to read and automatically complete checklists is severely restricted. The community is now debating whether or not to restore these features as a result of this development.
- **Voice Integration:** Checklists and procedures may be operated hands-free thanks to the Co-Pilot's voice integration capability. It enables pilots to focus on operating the aircraft while the co-pilot uses voice instructions to carry out standard chores. This makes the experience much more realistic and immersive. As an example, consider the third-party add-on Dynamic Virtual Co-Pilot for Checklists, which offers interactive in-flight operations and voice-activated checklist management.
- **Procedural Assistance:** This co-pilot then provides pilots with excellent direction for a variety of operations, including setup navigation, approach planning, and

starting. Pilots who are unfamiliar with certain aircraft systems or procedures would greatly benefit from this. Additionally, it provides visual signal highlighting in processes and detailed directions. By urging and directing through the aircraft's systems, such as IRS, the co-pilot may also be quite helpful in setting them.

+ **Emergency Procedures:** By providing checklists and instructions tailored to the particular emergency, the co-pilot will be able to assist the pilot in managing crucial circumstances during an emergency. Pilots may practice managing a variety of crises in the simulation environment, which greatly increases the realism of emergency training.

Putting Co-Pilot Features into Practice

The following actions will help you make the most of MSFS 2024's Co-Pilot features:

+ To access the Electronic Flight Bag, use the TAB key.
+ **Choose the Co-Pilot Option:** To access the capabilities and options that are accessible, go to the Co-Pilot area of the EFB.
+ **Configure Settings:** Adapt the Co-Pilot's preferences and degree of help to your need.
+ **Start Checklists and Procedures:** Start checklists, get procedural instructions, and handle emergency situations via the Co-Pilot's interface.

CHAPTER SEVENTEEN
INVESTIGATING INTERNATIONAL AIRPORTS AND SCENERIES

Finding Detailed Airports

With more than 150 meticulously constructed handmade airports that meticulously replicate their real-world counterparts, MSFS 2024 is the next quantum leap in airport modeling. **As shown below, a few of these airports are accessible in various editions:**

- There are 150 handmade airports in the Standard Edition and 155 in the Deluxe Edition.
- There are 160 individually designed airports in the Premium Deluxe and Aviator Editions.

London Heathrow Airport (EGLL), Frankfurt Airport (EDDF), Dubai International Airport (OMDB), San Francisco International Airport (KSFO), and Denver International Airport (KDEN) are a few examples. Accurate runways, taxiways, terminal buildings, and surrounding infrastructure are just a few examples of the meticulously designed airports. Each location's authenticity is enhanced with realistic lighting effects and high-resolution textures. Runway markers, taxi lines, and airport surfaces, for instance, are meticulously modeled, providing crisp, very realistic textures even at close range. From MSFS 2020 to MSFS 2024, handmade airports are often updated to maintain consistency and improve simulator experiences. Players who liked the previous version will now be able to experience improved, more realistic, and better-textured versions of their favorite airports.

Examining Sceneries around the World

However, MSFS 2024 offers a comprehensive worldwide scenic experience that extends beyond the airports. In addition to realistic water features and precisely recreated towns, the simulator's use of sophisticated photogrammetry and satellite data has allowed it to replicate the Earth's landscapes with amazing accuracy. The resolution of landscape data in various regions of the globe is shown on a color-coded global map. This tool will make low and slow VFR flying much more enjoyable by assisting users in locating the greatest ground scenery. The changing seasons and biomes feature further enhances the world's landscape. The transition between the seasons—from vivid, colorful fall to tranquil winter snowscapes—will be felt by the user, giving the virtual environment more authenticity and diversity.

Enhancing the Experience

There are many of options in the MSFS 2024 add-ons and modifications community for those who want even more out of their virtual flying experience. A vast collection of free landscape improvements, such as additional airports, airfields, and bush strips, may be found on websites like Flightsim.to. Numerous options for personalizing one's simulation environment are made possible by these user-developed add-ons. Additionally, new airports and very realistic landscapes are added by third-party merchants like Orbxt and iniBuilds. Orbx's Global Range, for instance, is a line of items that further improve this simulator's realism.

Recognizing Scenery Detail Levels (LOD)

The LOD system in MSFS 2024 regulates how the simulator updates the 3D models' textures and level of complexity. The complexity and richness of an item in the simulator are enhanced as an aircraft approaches it, adding more complex geometries and textures with better resolution. On the other hand, the simulator minimizes details as it gets further away from objects in order to save system resources and guarantee smooth operation.

Impact of Scenery and Performance

The simulator's performance and visual quality are greatly impacted by dynamic LOD modification. Highly detailed things like buildings, airports, and topographical features provide a realistic and engrossing experience when seen up close. However, over longer distances, the loss of detail aids in maintaining responsiveness and frame rates, both of which are critical for a smooth flying experience.

Modifying the LOD Configuration

Users may now adjust LOD settings based on their system capabilities thanks to MSFS 2024. By dragging sliders, the Settings menu allows you to adjust the simulator's TLOD and OLOD. Higher values improve the quality of distant objects and terrain, but they may also have an impact on performance, particularly on low-end computers. On the other hand, performance is enhanced at the expense of visual quality when these parameters are decreased.

LOD Optimization for Specific Systems

However, the best settings could differ based on the system being used. Feel free to adjust the parameters until you find a nice balance between performance and visual quality. These changes may be guided by system performance measures like frame rates and memory use.

Exploration with the Drone Camera

Without the limitations of real flying, the MSFS 2024 Drone Camera offers an enjoyable method to explore the virtual world. This mode allows for free-form exploration both on land and in the air, including across airports and within buildings. The skill is great for paying careful attention to little elements that could be seen in general landscape, cityscapes, and airports.

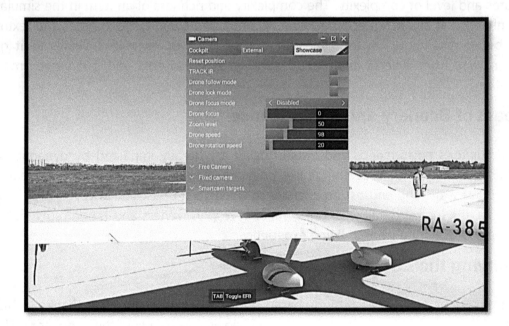

Turning on the drone's camera

Follow these steps to turn on the drone camera:

- To access the Toolbar, click the Drone symbol in the top portion of your screen. You may do this from the ground or while flying.
- **Access Showcase View:** To switch to this drone camera mode, choose Showcase from the drop-down menu.

- **Control the Camera:** A suitable controller or the keyboard may be used to control the camera. For example, the arrow keys change the direction the camera looks, while the WASD keys enable sideways movement. Use the Speed slider in the View menu to adjust the movement speed.

Examining Airports and the scenery

The drone camera works well for viewing landscapes and airports:
- **Airport Details:** To have a better grasp of the general layout of airports, users may see terminals, runways, and other amenities up close.
- **Cityscapes and Landmarks:** The camera examines metropolitan regions, historical sites, and natural marvels from a unique perspective.
- **Walkaround Mode:** For a better pre-flight lookaround, MSFS 2024 has included a "Walkaround" function that allows users to walk around their aircraft.

Advanced Functionalities

MSFS 2024 has improved the drone camera in a number of ways:
- **Walkaround Mode:** This feature allows customers to explore their aircraft in depth by walking around it.
- **Stream Deck Integration:** By combining the Drone Camera with gadgets like the Stream Deck, users may customize the controls to improve the exploring experience for those who prefer a more tactile engagement.

Community Perspectives

The MSFS community is very active in exchanging drone camera-related experiences and advice.
- **AVSIM Forum:** This forum offers insightful information and user experiences about the usage of drone cameras for scenic exploration.
- **Microsoft Flight Simulator Forums:** User-generated material is shown in threads devoted to the Drone Camera function, which also include instructions and advice.

Advice for Successful Exploration

To get the most out of the drone camera:
- **Modify Speed Settings:** To create a pleasant perspective, modify the movement speed based on the region being investigated.
- **Make use of camera presets:** Store certain camera settings or views in memory for easy access during later excursions.

﹢ **Combine with Walkaround Mode:** For a deeper exploration experience, the user may examine the aircraft's exterior and interior by using the Walkaround function.

Points of Interest (POI) Identification

Points of Interest are meticulously planned landmarks that provide MSFS 2024 realism and complexity. Famous structures, historical landmarks, bustling cities, and natural formations are all included in the POIs. Pilots can traverse and explore the planet with a greater feeling of immersion thanks to this integration of POIs.

Finding and Getting to Points of Interest

Understanding how to locate and access POIs inside the simulation is essential to maximizing their richness in MSFS 2024.

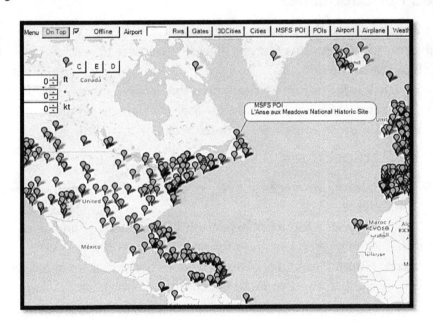

﹢ **Making POI Markers Active:**
  ➢ Navigate to the Options menu in the simulator.
  ➢ The 'Assistance' tab is then selected.
  ➢ This dropdown selection allows you to activate POI Markers, setting their state to 'On.'
  ➢ To facilitate exploration and navigation, the in-game map will provide symbols for various points of interest once activated.

153

- **Making Use of Interactive Maps:** Third-party programs, like the FStarter24 app, display interactive maps with handmade airports, 3D cities, and points of interest.In MSFS 2024, these maps also enable the aircraft to teleport to specified places for targeted study of certain noteworthy spots.
- **Examining Cities for Photogrammetry:** Cities for photogrammetry are included in MSFS 2024, where detailed 3D models of cityscapes are available. These are primarily designated as points of interest and provide plenty of chance to be flown over actual sites with remarkable precision.

Important Points of Interest to Investigate

MSFS 2024 has several points of interest worldwide. Some of the most noteworthy places to think about are as follows:

Indonesia's Pura Ulun Danu Bratan

This stunning water temple is situated on the beaches of Bali, Indonesia's Lake Bratan. It is a must-see point of interest because of its beautiful architecture and tranquil surroundings.

The Tin City, USA, Alaska

A remote Alaskan community renowned for its historical importance and distinctive architecture. A trip to this site will give you a great understanding of living in one of the world's most isolated regions.

The 3D Cities

New York, Paris, and Tokyo are just a few of the numerous photogrammetry cities that MSFS 2024 is delighted to offer, all of which are very detailed for flying and exploring.

Handmade Airports

The simulator offers a realistic representation of departures and arrivals thanks to its intricately detailed constructed airports. These are often found in locations where the majority of aviation activity takes place.

Japan's Mount Fuji

The famous Mount Fuji, seen from the pilot's perspective, has been meticulously captured. One of the most popular locations for sightseeing flights.

Improved Experience with Exploration

The following advice may help you enhance your investigation of MSFS 2024's POIs:

- **Make Use of the Drone Camera:** By allowing for a closer examination of the points of interest, the Drone Camera mode helps viewers appreciate the finer aspects of natural formations and monuments.
- **Take Part in Community Challenges:** Taking part in community challenges that highlight certain points of interest may provide organized chances for exploration and cultivate a feeling of accomplishment.
- **Stay Up:** Since new POIs and enhancements to the simulator are always being added, stay up with the most recent information from Asobo Studio and the MSFS community.

Changing the Scenery Settings

MSFS 2024 offers a wide variety of landscape modification options, from basic graphical adjustments to the addition of specially constructed airports and landmarks. It gives users a lot of options to improve speed, alter flying situations, and boost visual quality.

Launching the Scenery Editor

The MSFS 2024 Software Development Kit's Scenery Editor is the main tool for customizing scenery. With the help of this editor, users may alter the virtual world's scenery, add areas of interest, and construct airports, among other features. **The Scenery Editor may be opened by:**

- **Turn on Developer Mode:** Open the Options menu in the simulator and choose Developer Mode.
- Start the Scenery Editor: Choose Scenery Editor from the Tools menu in Dev Mode.

Keep in mind that the Scenery Editor must be used during a flight, not from the main menu, since it is intended for usage in simulation.

How to Make a Simple Scenery Project

Starting with a basic project is a good idea for those who are new to customizing landscape. Creating a new scenery package, adding objects, and modifying their attributes are all included in this.

Bringing in Personalized 3D Models

To add a unique building or landmark, one may import bespoke 3D models into the simulator.

To accomplish this;
- **Model Creation:** Make the model using a 3D modeling program such as Blender or 3DS Max.
- **Model Export:** Export the model in a glTF or other format that can be read by MSFS 2024.
- **Texture and Material Setup:** Configure the textures and materials to function correctly in the simulator's rendering engine.
- **Import into Scenery Editor:** To import the model and place it in the virtual environment, use the Scenery Editor.

Changing Scenery Graphical Settings

To strike a balance between performance and visual quality, MSFS 2024 offers the ability to modify graphical settings in addition to creating custom objects. **Among the primary settings are:**
- **Terrain Level of Detail:** Regulates the terrain mesh's level of detail.
- **Object Level of Detail:** Regulates how intricate 3D things are.
- **Texture Resolution:** This changes how crisp the textures of objects and the ground are.
- **Shadow Quality:** Regulates the shadows' distance and resolution.

Modifying them may significantly improve performance on systems with lesser specs or maximize visual quality on high-end hardware.

Considerations for Compatibility

One would want to know how their custom scenery functions in the new simulator when they go from MSFS 2020 to MSFS 2024. Custom scenery objects and associated texture files from MSFS 2020 generally function fine in MSFS 2024, however certain default library items may need to be updated or replaced because of changes to the simulator's architecture.

Personalized Scenery for MSFS 2024

- **Backup the Original Files:** For data safety, always make a backup of the original files before making any changes.
- **Incremental Test:** Make minor adjustments and assess performance and stability.
- **Keep Up to Date:** Check the SDK and community tools often for information on newly added features and enhancements.
- **Go Social:** Learn from others and share your experiences in discussion groups and forums.

CHAPTER EIGHTEEEN
TOOLS FOR FLIGHT PLANNING AND NAVIGATION

Making Use of the Integrated Flight Planner

You may access the primary flight planning tool online at https://planner.flightsimulator.com/. This web-based tool facilitates preparation on several devices and enables thorough flight planning outside the simulator. Furthermore, the in-sim EFB ensures flexibility during flight operations by offering flight planning capabilities from inside the cockpit.

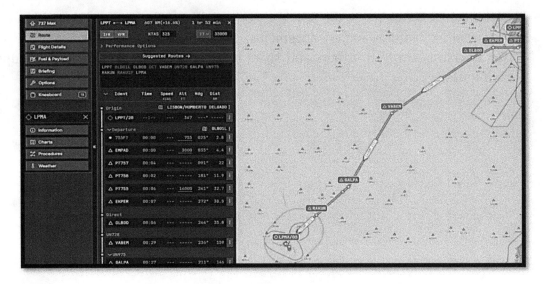

Comprehending the Interface

⬥ An interactive map and a number of choices are shown when the flight planner is opened.
  ➢ **Map Presets:** Modify the screen to accommodate different kinds of flights:
  ➢ Instrument flights over 18,000 feet are referred to as IFR High.
  ➢ Instrumental flights below 18,000 feet are referred to as IFR Low.
  ➢ **VFR:** Visual Flights, which place more emphasis on landmarks and landscape.
⬥ **Turn the following overlays on or off to alter what appears on the map:**
  ➢ **Airports:** Select whether to display or conceal airports.

> ➤ **Nav Aids:** Activate and deactivate the display of navigational aids, including airways, NDBs, and VORs.
> ➤ **Waypoints:** Turn on and off enroute and terminal waypoints.
> ➤ **Airspaces:** Restricted and regulated airspace borders on-screen.
> ➤ **Weather:** Shows the current conditions, wind, precipitation, and cloud cover.
> ➤ **Landmarks:** Draw attention to significant natural and man-made features.

Pilots can retain situational awareness, observe aviation regulations, and design flight plans for particular requirements with the help of these technologies.

Making a Flight Plan for VFR

When the weather is favorable, VFR flight plans work well because the pilot may use external visual cues to guide the aircraft.

- **Selecting departing and Arrival Points:** Find and choose your departing airport using the search box. Next, decide the airport you want to go to.
- **Route Planning:** The planner creates a straight line connecting the two locations if flying directly. Click on the map to manually construct waypoints or particular locations, if any.
- **Airspace Awareness:** To adhere to aviation laws, use the airspace overlay to identify any restricted or regulated airspaces along the flight route.
- **Weather Considerations:** To ascertain where an alternate could be necessary, turn on the weather overlay and examine the current circumstances along your route.
- **Save the Flight Plan:** Save the flight plan if you're satisfied. You may import the file when you set up pre-flight or load it into MSFS 2024 via the EFB.

Making a Flight Plan for IFR

For instrument navigation in bad weather and particularly in controlled airspace, the IFR flight plan is a crucial tool.

- **Select Airports of Departure and Arrival:** Locate and select the airports of departure and destination.
- **Choose SIDs and STARs:** Standard Terminal Arrival Routes (STARs) and Standard Instrument Departures (SIDs) improve traffic flow. To ensure adherence to air traffic control regulations, choose the proper procedures according to your airport.
- **Enroute Navigation:** Define your route by adding airways and waypoints. The optimal routes may be recommended by the flight planner based on current weather and air traffic.

- **Altitude Planning:** Using conventional IFR altitude assignments, determine cruising altitudes appropriate for your aircraft and flight direction.
- **Reviewing and Saving:** Verify the correctness of the whole route, ensuring that all processes and waypoints have been included correctly. The flight plan may be saved and loaded into the simulator whenever you want.

EFB-Based In-Sim Integration

In MSFS 2024, the EFB is a flexible instrument for in-flight monitoring and adjustments:
- **Loading Flight Plans:** The EFB provides immediate access to stored flight plans, allowing for smooth planning and execution transitions.
- **Real-time weather updates:** To ensure efficiency and safety, keep an eye on the current weather and modify your flight itinerary as necessary.
- **Navigational Charts:** To help with situational awareness and navigation, access approach plates, enroute charts, and airport diagrams.
- **Performance Calculations:** Use the EFB to determine important performance metrics, such takeoff and landing distances for operational safety.

By giving pilots access to vital information, the incorporation of EFB improves in-flight decision-making.

Extra Features

- **Bringing in External Flight Schedules:**
  - ➢ To improve interoperability with third-party programs that are used on a daily basis by the majority of flight simulation fans, Flight Planner further permits the importation of route plans from other sources, such as SimBrief or Navigraph. The whole planning process may be streamlined by allowing the user to export flight plans in appropriate formats, such as.pln, and then import them into MSFS 2024.
  - ➢ **User-Defined Custom Waypoints and Routes:** This feature enables experienced users to design unique waypoints for accurate navigation according to a certain flying situation or difficulty. For mission-based flying or simulating real-world situations, this is really helpful.
  - ➢ **Air Traffic Control (ATC) Integration:** Flight plans made using the built-in planner are immediately synced with the in-sim ATC system to facilitate communication and ensure that directives from ATC are followed. This makes the flight plans seem very genuine.

161

The Best Ways to Utilize the Integrated Flight Planner

- **Start Planning Early:** Long before your simulator session begins; create your flight path using the web-based planner. This guarantees that every aspect is taken into account and permits a more relaxed preparation process.
- **Make Use of Real-World Data:** MSFS 2024's planner uses navigational and meteorological data as of right now. To improve realism, make use of this by turning on overlays and cross-referencing with actual aviation charts.
- **Play with Features:** Get to know all the tools at your disposal, such as enroute choices, airspace overlays, and SID/STAR selection. Practice with these features will lead to efficiency and confidence.
- **Verify your Plan:** Before saving and loading the aircraft, make sure your plan accounts for any conflicts like as restricted airspace, incorrect waypoints, or mismatched heights.
- **Adjust While Flying:** Although MSFS 2024's flight planner is extensive, unforeseen adjustments may be made in midair. Make real-time modifications without interfering with your operation by using the in-sim EFB.

Including Navigation Tools from Third Parties

The navigation and flight planning features in Microsoft Flight Simulator 2024 have been enhanced, giving pilots a more realistic flying experience. The incorporation of third-party navigation tools, which give far more data and functionality than the default simulator, is one of the most significant enhancements.

Integration of Navigraphs

When it comes to giving flight simulation enthusiasts access to real-world navigation data and charts, Navigraph has been in the forefront. Because of the smooth integration of Navigraph's services for MSFS 2024, pilots may now obtain the most recent navigation data received from Jeppesen straight from the simulator. This ensures that the airways, navaids, terminal procedures, and geographical coordinates of all in-sim aircraft—including those installed as third-party add-ons—are correct and updated with each AIRAC cycle. In-game, this connectivity extends to the Electronic Flight Bag, where pilots may plan their flights using SimBrief and Navigraph Charts. Pilots may now plan and execute flights with real-world precision thanks to this feature, which makes the experience even more realistic and seamless.

Integration of SimBrief

Perhaps the most popular flight-planning product on the market, SimBrief incorporates its features fully within the EFB for MSFS 2024. This implies that pilots may create comprehensive flight plans from inside the simulator, including route, fuel calculations, and weather forecasts. Overall, it aids in flight planning as the link will guarantee that flight plans in MSFS 2024 and the simulator are more accurately reflected.

Limited compatibility with Navmap

With several capabilities for the virtual pilot, Little Navmap is a free and open-source flight planning and navigation program. Some users have complained about issues importing flight plans, such as the simulator altering or rejecting approaches, even though it is compatible with MSFS 2024. These differences highlight a crucial point about the simulator's ability to work with third-party applications for precise flight planning and execution.

Obstacles and Things to Think About

There are several difficulties with third-party navigation tools linked with MSFS 2024. The potential disparity between the simulator's default navigation data and that from third-party programs is likely the most significant. These variations may result in irregularities in navigation and flight planning, which might compromise the simulation's accuracy and realism. The technological problems of integration provide further hurdles. For instance, it could be necessary to modify the simulator's code in order to override its default capabilities in order to integrate proprietary GPS products into the autopilot system. These changes may get intricate and may potentially affect the simulator's performance and stability.

Comprehending Airway Routing

Airways are established flight paths that airplanes adhere to in order to travel between destinations in a safe and effective manner. Similar to how highways direct automobiles, airplanes direct pilots on designated courses. **Two types of airways exist:**
- **Victor Airways:** Victor Airways is the name of the airline that begins with the letter "V" and a number, such V12. The Victor Airways is located below 18,000 feet, which is the typical altitude at which transportation takes place.
- **Jet Flight Routes:** These are flights that are operated at altitudes higher than 18,000 feet and are identified by the letter "J" followed by a number, such J45.

By linking many waypoints, including GPS locations, NDBs (Non-Directional Beacons), and VORs (VHF Omnidirectional Range stations), these airways form a network that allows pilots to conduct IFR flights.

MSFS 2024's Airway Routing System

A new, sophisticated flight planning feature in MSFS 2024 enables the virtual pilot to highly integrate airway routing into the flight plan. For increased flexibility and **accessibility, the simulator gives users a lot of options between an online Web-based planner and an in-sim flight planner.**

- **In-Sim Flight Planner:** Pilots may use this tool, which is instantly available inside the simulator, to build flight plans by choosing airways, waypoints, and departure and arrival airports. A three-dimensional representation of the route is provided by the in-sim planner, which enhances situational awareness.
- **Online Flight Planner:** This comprehensive web program allows MSFS 2024 users to plan flights, including real-world airway data. It may be accessed online at planner.flightsimulator.com. Users may use the program to plan flights outside of the simulator and then import them into MSFS 2024.

Formulating a Flight Plan Based on Airways

You may use Airways to generate a flight plan in MSFS 2024 by following the procedures shown below:

- **Launch the Flight Planner Website:** You may use the online flight planner or the one that is included within the simulation.
- **Choose the Arrival and Departure Airports:** Enter the names of the airports you want to arrive at and leave from.
- **Select International Flight Rules:** You will be able to access the different airway route choices when you have chosen IFR as your flight rules.
- **Including Waypoints and Airways on the Map:**
  - ➤ **Manual input:** By manually entering certain waypoints and choosing the airways that match them, you may construct your route using manual input.
  - ➤ **Auto-Generated Routes:** Make use of the planner's auto-routing function to create an ideal route that incorporates the necessary airways.
- **Examine and Adjust the Route:** Examine the recommended path to ensure that it aligns with your flying goals. Make any required modifications, such as adding or deleting airways or waypoints.
- **Export and Load the Flight Plan:** To enable execution, save the flight plan and import it into MSFS 2024. The export and load procedure is this.

Benefits of Airway Routing Use

The following are a few benefits of utilizing airways while arranging your flights:
- **Realism:** The fact that you will be following recognized airways, which are a representation of actual aviation activities, will further increase the simulation's realism.
- **Efficiency:** Airlines are designed to provide quick routes between destinations, which may cut down on both the duration of travel and the quantity of fuel used.
- **Safety:** The usage of airways may help ensure safety by keeping one safe from other aircraft and navigational hazards.

Advanced Functionalities and Features

MSFS 2024's flight planning tools include a number of cutting-edge features that will help with airway routing, such as:
- **Realtime Weather Integration:** It's a great idea to take into account the present weather while planning a route. This enables adjustments to be made if the weather turns out to be unfavorable via active airways.
- **Navigational Charts:** To make sure you adhere to the protocols established to manage air traffic, view comprehensive charts such as Standard Instrument Departures (SIDs) and Standard Terminal Arrival Routes (STARs).
- **3D Route Visualization:** By allowing you to see your chosen route in three dimensions, you can better comprehend topographical issues and altitude variations along the airways that the flight path will traverse.

Practical Advice on Airway Routing

- **Keep Up to Date:** As airways change and adapt, your simulators navigation data should be updated to reflect these changes.
- **Cross-Check with Real-World Data:** A pilot may assess accuracy and realism by comparing real-world data with an existing flight plan.
- **Practice with Various Scenarios:** To begin refining your airway routing abilities inside MSFS 2024, experiment with different routes, weather, and aircraft.

How to Determine Fuel Needs

Considering all possible factors and unforeseen circumstances, it is crucial to do a precise fuel estimate in order to guarantee that an aircraft will be able to safely finish its planned journey. **The following are the main elements that go into fuel planning:**
- Fuel used for ground operations, such as engine start-up, runway taxiing, and any delays before to takeoff, is referred to as taxi fuel.

- **Trip Fuel:** The quantity of fuel needed to complete the journey from the airport of departure to the airport of destination while adhering to the flight plan's parameters, which include the predicted altitudes, speeds, and weather.
- The extra amount of gasoline that accounts for unforeseen circumstances, such deviating from the intended trajectory, last-minute weather changes, or directives from the air traffic control tower, is known as contingency fuel. More than 5% of the trip fuel or five minutes of holding at 1,500 feet above the destination airport should be the minimum amount of contingency fuel needed. The International Civil Aviation Organization's (ICAO) Annex 6 states that this amount is determined using the projected arrival weight.
- **Alternate Fuel:** The fuel required to fly from the destination airport to a backup airport in the event that landing at the destination airport is not feasible.
- The amount of fuel that has to be saved as a reserve after landing is known as the final reserve fuel. For airplanes with piston engines, this is usually interpreted as 45 minutes of endurance speed flying time. If a pilot has less gasoline than the last reserve, they must declare an emergency, commonly known as Mayday gasoline.
- **Extra Fuel:** Any more fuel needed on the ground that is judged essential based on unique operational factors, including prolonged holding patterns, anticipated delays, or any other flight-specific oddities.

How to Determine Fuel Needs

The following fuel needs may be precisely estimated by virtual pilots using the technologies included in MSFS 2024:

- **Integrated Flight Planning System:** Information about certain flight parameters, such as aircraft model, route, altitude, and anticipated weather, may be entered into the simulator's flight planning interface. It calculates the expected amount of gasoline that will be used for the whole trip based on these parameters.
- **Web-Based Flight Planner:** Microsoft has released a web-based flight planner that can be accessed using tablet or PC browsers. Users may schedule flights outside of the simulator using this functionality. This service makes flight planning simpler and more thorough by giving users access to radio navigation data, aviation charts, and weather information.
- **Electronic Flight Bag (EFB):** A significant portion of the MSFS 2024 default aircraft are equipped with an EFB, which offers a number of functions including as fuel calculation, weight and balance verification, and real-time flight data monitoring. All aircraft may use this functionality since the EFB can be accessed via the user interface that is included in the game.

Useful Procedures for Fuel Calculation

To calculate the amount of gasoline required for MSFS 2024:

- **Determine Trip Fuel:** Using the flight planning tools, determine how much fuel will be required for the trip and choose the best course of action, taking into consideration the aircraft's performance, altitude, and wind speed. An estimate of the quantity of gasoline needed for this trip will be generated by the system.
- **Add Contingency Fuel:** The International Civil Aviation Organization (ICAO) recommends supplying at least 5% of the trip fuel or five minutes of holding fuel at a height of 1,500 feet above the destination in order to prepare for unforeseen circumstances.
- **Determine the gasoline for the Alternate Airport:** If you must land at a different airport, you must use the same techniques you used to determine the gasoline you will need to fly from your destination to the other airport.
- **Add Final Reserve Fuel:** Make sure that, for piston-engine-powered aircraft, or the amount given for the kind of aircraft being simulated, there will be at least 45 minutes of fuel left at the conclusion of the flight.
- **Consider other gasoline needs:** Take into account any extra circumstances, such as anticipated delays, holding, or particular operating needs, that would necessitate the use of more gasoline.

Regulatory Aspects

Pilots must be aware of the constraints of fuel planning in both the real and virtual worlds. In addition to allowing for thirty minutes of additional fuel during the day or forty-five minutes during the night on each trip, pilots of VFR flights are required to plan enough fuel to fly to the target landing destination while taking wind and weather conditions into account. The regulations are much more stringent if the flight is IFR. Furthermore, these trips often call for extra reserves and gasoline for a different airport.

Flight Plans: Importing and Exporting

Using Microsoft Flight Planning System 2024 to Export and Import Flight Plans

Making a flight plan is quite simple with MSFS 2024 due to the overhaul of the flight planning interface. The flight plan may be exported after a route has been charted so that it can be shared with the community or used in applications outside of the flight simulation community.

You may export a flight plan by:
- **Plan your Route:** Choose the airports of departure and arrival, as well as the waypoints and protocols you want to adhere to, using the in-sim flight planner.
- **Save Flight Plan:** Verify that this function is enabled in MSFS after using the flight planner to trace the route. MSFS 2024 flight plans, which include a considerable variety of tools for flight planning and add-on support, are to be stored in the.pln format.
- **Choose the Save place:** Decide on a place for the file's storage. Ensure that the.pln file is in a directory on your computer so that it can be readily accessible for use or sharing later.

Additionally, the exported.pln file may be shared with other pilots for additional study or loaded into compatible avionics suites. Additionally, it may be used for planning in third-party applications such as SimBrief or Little Navmap.

Flight Plan Importation into MSFS 2024

The adaptability of MSFS 2024 is increased by its interoperability with external flight planning tools. A flight plan may be imported by:
- **Obtain the Flight Plan:** Verify that the flight plan is in the.pln file format. This format may be used to export flight plans using programs like SimBrief and Little Navmap.
- **Load the Flight Plan:** To complete the route on the World Map, choose the 'Load' option in the World Map interface, go to the location where the.pln file has been stored, and then load the file.
- **Review and Modify:** Examine the flight plan in the simulator after loading. Verify that all procedures, waypoints, and other information match the flight you wish to take. Make any required adjustments to account for current weather conditions, aircraft traffic, or individual preferences.

Complex flight plans benefit greatly from this feature, which enables thorough preparation in external applications and flawless implementation inside MSFS 2024.

Connecting Third-Party Tools

Support for third-party flight planning software substantially expanded MSFS 2024's adaptability. More sophisticated options for flight planning and exporting a flight plan compatible with MSFS 2024 are available in applications like Navigraph Charts and SimBrief. For example, Navigraph allows users to plan flights and export them straight to the simulator, ensuring that in-sim navigation and pre-flight preparation are consistent.

Best Practices and Considerations

Although the import and export features are strong, take into account the following:

- **Compatibility:** MSFS 2024 must be able to use the flight plan format. Although the.pln format is the industry standard, it is advised to verify compatibility with certain aircraft avionics.
- **Data Accuracy:** Verify that all waypoints, airways, and procedures are read accurately when importing flight plans. Discrepancies may sometimes arise, particularly when utilizing outdated navigation data or on complex routes.
- **In-Flight Modifications:** Be ready to make modifications in real time. The aircraft may need to veer from the intended course due to circumstances like weather conditions, airspace constraints, or directives from air traffic control.

CHAPTER NINETEEN
DEBUGGING AND ASSISTANCE

Fixing Typical Technical Problems

With its amazing sense of realism and expanded functionality, Microsoft Flight Simulator 2024 has really captured the hearts and minds of aviation aficionados. **Technical difficulties may arise with any complicated program and this section attempts to address some of them and provide fixes for a more enjoyable flight.**

- **Prolonged loading periods:** The lengthy time it takes for MSFS 2024 to open has drawn complaints from a lot of users. One of the likely reasons might be the system clock being out of sync. Correctly setting the date and time of your system will undoubtedly cut the startup time by an order of magnitude. This may be resolved by synchronizing your system clock with an online time server.

- **High Menu CPU/GPU Usage:** Some users have noticed that menu navigation increases CPU and GPU use, which might result in system overheating. Consider turning on V-Sync or establishing a frame rate cap in the game's graphical options to lessen this. During menu navigation, this method might stop the hardware from generating frames needlessly.

- **Issues with Control Binding:** Control binding issues have been plaguing certain users, causing some inputs to simply not react or function as intended. The first step in fixing this is to confirm that your pedals, yokes, and joysticks are connected and recognized by the system correctly. Next, verify that all controls are allocated appropriately in the game's control options. Try resetting the control profiles to their default settings and then reassigning them if that doesn't work.

- **Unnoticeable Mouse Cursor:** The ability to move about the simulator is hampered by an invisible or absent mouse pointer. Conflicts with connected devices or the game's display settings may be the cause of the issue. Switching between windowed and full-screen modes may sometimes bring the pointer back into view. Additionally, verify whether the issue is resolved by disconnecting and replugging your input devices.

- **The Cockpit Controls Are Unusable:** According to some users, it might be challenging to draw attention to and interact with hotspots. This is often a cockpit interaction system setting. MSFS 2024 has a number of interaction modes, including "Legacy" and "Lock." Switching between them in the Accessibility settings might improve the quality of the interactions.

- **Not Able to Remove the Co-Pilot:** The inability to remove the co-pilot from the cockpit view has been a source of complaints from certain customers. Usually, this is resolved by adjusting the crew settings and gaining access to aircraft customization options before to a trip. To leave the right side unoccupied throughout the flight, make sure the co-pilot option is not selected.

- **Mouse Sensitivity Variability:** The simulation may be ruined by inconsistent mouse sensitivity, especially during the free look. A more reliable and pleasant input response may be obtained by modifying the mouse sensitivity levels in the game's control options. You may improve control by adjusting these parameters to your liking.

- **Absence of Offline Mode:** Since there isn't yet a completely offline option, MSFS 2024 mostly relies on internet streaming for its real-time data and globe pictures. However, the simulator does allow you to explicitly cache areas. Better performance is eventually provided in places with high traffic volumes by downloading and storing data there, which lessens the need for real-time streaming.

- **Unable to Turn off ATC:** Although it might be difficult to turn off ATC communications, some users would rather fly without ATC direction. Although there isn't a simple option to disable ATC, most ATC interactions may be disabled or eliminated by turning off AI ATC help and refraining from contacting ATC while flying.

- **Preserving Flight Configurations:** There is no direct option to store certain flight configurations, and the existing system mostly depends on recent flights for fast access. As a solution, think about manually recording the specifics of your desired flight configurations, such as the aircraft, airports of departure and arrival, weather, and other pertinent parameters, so that you may replicate them as required.

- **Default Time of Day Configurations:** As of right now, MSFS 2024 is unable to establish a default flight time of day. Every time you fly, you will need to configure it to your liking.

- **Problems with Streaming and Server Connectivity:** Scenery loading is either absent or very delayed as a consequence. These kinds of problems are often caused by server connection or Internet capacity. Make sure your connection is steady to improve streaming, and a wired connection will help your system be more dependable. Additionally, experimenting with several DNS servers, such as those offered by Cloudflare or Google, can enhance connection.

- **Aircraft and Missing Content:** There have been reports of missing flights and other material, mostly due to cache problems or busy servers. Usually, emptying the rolling cache in the game's settings fixes it. To ensure that all the files are installed successfully, try reinstalling the specific content or aircraft using the content manager if it doesn't work.

+ **Desktop crashes (CTDs):** It's annoying when the desktop crashes. Outdated drivers and other software/hardware problems are the typical suspects. A decent, current graphics driver and Windows update are essential. To assist avoid issues with the simulator; turn off any background program that isn't necessary. If the problems continue, event viewer logs may be reviewed to learn more about the reason, which can aid with more troubleshooting.

+ **Resources for the Community and Support"** For ongoing assistance and to find out about known problems and changes, see the Zendesk support website and the official Microsoft Flight Simulator forums. Interacting with the community may provide more knowledge and solutions from simmers that may have encountered and resolved a problem before.

Using the Official Support Channels

Microsoft Flight Simulator 2024 technical problems might be a little annoying, but you can obtain the assistance you want by using the appropriate support channels. **Here's how to efficiently use these resources:**

+ **Support Website for Microsoft Flight Simulator:** The Microsoft Flight Simulator Support Website is the main location for official assistance. It has an extensive knowledge library that includes articles, frequently asked topics, and instructions for fixing common problems. Use its built-in search function to look for answers to your problems.

+ **Obtaining In-Game Assistance:** Navigate to the 'Help' or 'Support' sections while playing the game; they are often found on the main menu. In addition to providing connections to support websites, this page sometimes enables instant help for common problems without requiring users to leave the gaming environment.

+ **Support for Microsoft:** The Microsoft Support website is particularly helpful for problems that are not covered by the Flight Simulator support site. Support is available for more general problems with Microsoft accounts, billing inquiries, and technical difficulties with the Windows operating system.

+ **Support for Xbox:** The Xbox Support website is helpful for problems pertaining to consoles, network connection, and Xbox Live services whether you are using the Xbox or playing on it.

+ **Forums for Communities:** Interaction with the community might sometimes be advantageous. The Microsoft Flight Simulator forums are quite active and include anything from gameplay and personal experiences to troubleshooting questions. Before posing a new question, use the search option to see whether your issue has previously been resolved.

- **Channels for Social Media:** Microsoft Flight Simulator maintains active social media profiles and posts regular news, updates, and support details. By following them, you may stay informed about known problems or fixes.
- **Send in a Ticket:** It will be in your best interest to open a support request if you are unable to resolve your issue using the resources that are provided. 'Submit a Request' is an option on the Microsoft Flight Simulator Support Website. Remember to provide thorough details about your issue, system specifications, error messages, and how to replicate the situation. They will be more equipped to identify and address your issue with this information.
- **Verify the status of the server:** Occasionally, the server side may be the problem. Prior to any extensive troubleshooting, confirm that there are no ongoing maintenance or outages that might affect gaming services on the Xbox Status page.
- **Maintain Up-to-Date Software:** Update your operating system, drivers, and Microsoft Flight Simulator 2024. Numerous updates provide speed improvements and fixes for recognized problems. Check often using your system settings and the in-game launcher.
- **Give Input:** It is beneficial for the developers if you provide feedback if you run across a new issue or have ideas for enhancements. Please share your experience using the official forums or in-game feedback features. Feedback that is constructive aids in the simulator's continuous improvement.

Using Resources and Community Forums

The purpose of the official Microsoft Flight Simulator forums is community engagement, support, and conversation. Here, you may interact with other simmers, look for support, or exchange stories. **There are categories in the forum area dedicated to the following:**

- Official information and announcements about the Microsoft Flight Simulator.
- User-generated material, including tutorials, videos, and screenshots, may be found and shared on the Community material Hangar.
- **Discussion Hub:** Talk about primary or external features and goods.
- **User Support Hub:** Ask other users for assistance with any issues you're having.
- **Bug Reporting Hub:** Only report issues with first-party content and the main simulator.

These forums are regulated, controlled spaces where people may look for answers and exchange ideas.

Online AVSIM

With forums, file libraries, and product evaluations, AVSIM is among the oldest communities for fans of flight simulation. It is a volunteer-run, non-profit organization that provides access to a wealth of data and flight simulator accessories. There are special areas on the AVSIM Forums for Microsoft Flight Simulator 2020 and 2024 where users may talk about anything, exchange tips, and resolve issues.

The r/flightsim community on Reddit

The r/flightsim group on Reddit is a thriving community for flight simulation. People go there to ask questions, exchange stories, and provide support to one another. People submit inquiries in megathreads concerning unofficial support, and the community responds by offering assistance when it can.

Discussions in the Steam Community

The Steam Community Discussions website is an excellent resource for anybody who purchased MSFS 2024 on Steam. Topic-specific forums such as General Discussion, Aircraft & Systems, and Install Performance & Graphics are included. It is a helpful forum for troubleshooting and assistance because users exchange thoughts, solutions, and experiences.

Forums for Orbx Community and Support

One of the most well-known creators of flight simulation sceneries and add-ons is Orbx. This is the location of the Microsoft Flight Simulator 2024 subforum. For MSFS 2024 users, this peer-to-peer network that discusses Orbx goods looks for and offers help.

Forums on FlightSim.Com

FlightSim.Com is another well-known site in the flight simulation community. Forums, file libraries, and information regarding the majority of flight simulators, including MSFS 2024, are accessible via it. Users may seek for assistance, exchange advice, and debate many subjects on the forums.

Advice for Making Use of Community Resources

- **Before posting, search:** A lot of questions could have previously been addressed. Look for discussions about your issue by using the search function.
- **Give Detailed Information:** When asking for help, be as specific as possible about your system, the issue you're having, and the actions you've made so far. This will enable others to provide you with the best possible assistance.
- Be kind, patient, and polite: Volunteers and other enthusiasts assist with the community forums. Recognize that replies won't come right away and treat encounters with patience and respect.
- Give Something Back: Share with the community any solutions you discover to issues you're encountering. People in similar situations may benefit from your experiences.

Common Problems and Local Remedies

MSFS 2024 had various technical problems within a week or two after its debut, such as users reporting being stuck at 97% loading. A user also offered a likely fix, which involves fixing the simulator and then reinstalling it using the system settings. Strange malfunctions in the simulator have also been reported. In order to verify that all necessary system files are present and undamaged, a community debate recommended using the DISM and SFC tools to examine the Windows installation's integrity.

Reporting Issues and Offering Input

Together with helpful criticism, these problems contribute to the simulator's continuous growth and enhancement.

How Microsoft Flight Simulator Bugs Are Reported

The actions:
- **Verify the Issue:** Before reporting, confirm that the issue isn't due to a system constraint or a user mistake. To be sure the problem is constant, reproduce it.
- **Examine Previous Reports:** To find out whether the problem has been reported before, go through the Microsoft Flight Simulator Forums. In addition to avoiding duplicate reports, this will allow you to vote on current concerns and highlight their importance.
- **Obtain Comprehensive Information:** Compile thorough information on the problem, such as:

- ➢ **Description:** Clearly state the problem and provide instructions on how to replicate it.
- ➢ **System Specifications:** Give details about your software and hardware setup.
- ➢ **Videos or screenshots:** Visual proof is often quite helpful.
- ➢ **Log Files:** Provide pertinent logs to help developers identify the issue.
- ✦ **Send in the Report:** Kindly send in your research in the official forums' MSFS 2024 Bug Reports area. Make sure your report is concise, straightforward, and devoid of extraneous details.
- ✦ **Follow-Up:** If someone replies or requests further information, follow up on your report if needed. To resolve issues effectively, have positive conversations with consumers and developers.

Giving Microsoft Flight Simulator Feedback

The foundation of whatever development MSFS 2024 undertakes is constructive criticism. To provide constructive criticism:
- ✦ **Use Official Channels:** Share your thoughts and experiences on the Microsoft Flight Simulator Forums. It would enable the developers to establish objectives for product enhancement and keep them updated on community reaction.
- ✦ **Be detailed and constructive:** Clearly state your opinions while concentrating on certain traits or elements. Instead of just pointing out problems, provide recommendations about how to make things better.
- ✦ **Be Social:** Engage in conversations, vote, and complete surveys to provide general input on the simulator's functionality and performance.
- ✦ **Stay Up to Date:** Make sure to patch and stay current. If certain issues persist after upgrades, submit them for more work.

Obstacles and Community Perspectives

Numerous problems, including server overloads and technological hiccups, have plagued the MSFS 2024 deployment. For instance, several gamers complain about crashes, missing airplanes, and lengthy loading times. These issues were recognized by the developers, who have been attempting to fix them. People have been sharing their experiences, reporting issues, and providing comments on the community forums, which have been quite busy. The effectiveness of bug reporting and the responsiveness of developers are topics of discussion. While some users express annoyance about unsolved problems, others value the creators' efforts to address difficulties.

Maintaining Simulator Updates

The cloud-based streaming paradigm that MSFS 2024 currently uses greatly minimizes the footprint of the installation and enables on-demand data streaming. With this technique, there is no need for laborious manual downloads of large files, and the simulator may always be updated with new scenery, aircraft, and features.

Looking for Updates

Make sure your simulator is up to date by doing the following:
- Open MSFS 2024 on your PC or Xbox Series X/S to start the simulator.
- **Open the Main Menu:** Open the main menu when the simulator has loaded.
- **Check for Updates:** When the simulator first starts up, it automatically looks for updates. You will be asked to download and install any updates that are available.
- **Manual Check:** The "Updates" section is always available in the Settings or Options menu, so you may check yourself if you think an update hasn't been done.

Resolving Update Problems

Users may have problems while upgrading. The typical ones are:
- **Installation Stucks:** Usually on certain percentages, updates may hold up or get stuck. Issues with local connection or server load might be the cause.
- **Missing Content:** Some terrain or aircraft may not appear in the simulator after upgrading.
- **Errors or crashes:** During or after an upgrade, the simulator may crash or display error messages.

How to Fix Update Problems

- To restart the simulator, shut down MSFS 2024 completely and then relaunch it. This often resolves little issues.
- **Verify Server Status:** To find out whether there are any server problems right now, check the official Microsoft Flight Simulator forums or help website. High server load may sometimes impact how updates work.
- **Verify Your Internet:** Please confirm that you have a reliable and strong enough internet connection to download updates.
- **Clean Cache:** Issues that can be related to corrupted data will be resolved by the simulator's clean cache technique. Usually, the settings menu has the option.

- **Repair Installation:** Try fixing the simulator using the program settings on your computer if the issues continue. Go to Settings > Applications > Microsoft Flight Simulator 2024 > Advanced Settings > Repair on Windows.
- **Simulator Reinstallation:** After uninstalling the application, reinstall MSFS 2024 as a last resort and only in extreme circumstances (if everything else fails). Save all of your downloaded tweaks and changes ahead of time.

Keeping Up to Date

Periodically, Asobo Studio and Microsoft provide live updates that improve application performance and fix many issues. On December 12, 2024, Patch 3 (v1.2.7.0) went online, resolving hundreds of issues and more. **For the most recent version news:**
- **Official Forums:** Join the community on the official Microsoft Flight Simulator forums to discuss problems and solutions.
- **Development Updates:** Stay informed about upcoming patches and hotfixes by following the official development updates, which are released on a regular basis.
- **Social Media:** For updates and assistance in real time, follow the official social media accounts.

Community Assistance

The MSFS community is very helpful and active. You may wish to contact your fellow simmers if you're having any problems:
- **Reddit:** For assistance and troubleshooting, the subreddits r/flightsim and r/MicrosoftFlightSim are particularly helpful.
- **AVSIM Forums:** An elderly community where individuals may exchange solutions and experiences.
- **Discord Servers:** For instant communication and help, the majority of MSFS groups have a Discord server.

CHAPTER TWENTY
IMPROVING YOUR EXPERIENCE WITH SIMULATION

Constructing a Home Cockpit

Creating a home cockpit configuration for Microsoft Flight Simulator 2024 can significantly improve your simulation experience and make it much more realistic and immersive. **Here is a thorough section to assist you in setting up a productive home cockpit:**

- **Establish Your Goals and Spending Limit:** Prior to investing in any equipment, establish your objectives. Will you be taking your training seriously, maybe in preparation for a genuine license, or will you be flying just for fun? Or are you interested in doing both? The complexity and cost of the setup depend on your objectives. Establish a budget based on your requirements. An entry-level setup costs around $450, while the most expensive systems cost well over $3,000.

- **Select the Proper Hardware:** A simple home cockpit includes:
  - **Computer System:** A strong PC is necessary for MSFS 2024 to run well. It is strongly advised that your system specs match or beyond the game's suggested specifications.
  - **Flight Controls:** Depending on the kind of aircraft you choose, you may choose between a joystick and a yoke.
  - **Entry-Level:** With an integrated throttle and twist grip, the Logitech Extreme 3D Pro offers a smooth pitch and roll axis.
  - **Mid-Range:** For an even more engaging experience, the Thrustmaster TCA Sidestick Airbus Edition simulates the sidestick seen in modern Airbus aircraft.
  - **High-end:** For serious pilots, Honeycomb Alpha Flight Controls Yoke and Bravo Throttle Quadrant provide realistic yoke and throttle quadrant.
  - **Rudder pedals:** These are optional, although they improve control and provide a little realism.
  - **Throttle Quadrant:** For serious flying, particularly in multi-engine aircraft, having a separate throttle quadrant is excellent for keeping an eye on the engines.
  - **Visual Displays:** A wider field of vision may be achieved with a high-resolution display or many monitors. For a more engaging experience, some fans choose ultra-wide displays or curved monitors.

- ➢ **Audio System:** Good speakers or a microphone-equipped headset may enhance communication and situational awareness.
- ✦ **Create the layout for the cockpit:** Make sure your equipment is set up to resemble a genuine cockpit. Think about the following:
  - ➢ **Ergonomics:** Make sure your sitting arrangement is comfortable for prolonged periods of time and that all controls are easily accessible.
  - ➢ **Frame and Mounts:** Your controllers and displays may be safely held in place by a strong frame. While some aficionados buy pre-made frames, others construct their own.
  - ➢ **Instrument Panels:** You may use software to show simulated instruments on extra displays or install real instrument panels for a more realistic effect.
- ✦ **Install and Set up Software:** It's time to install MSFS 2024 and allow it to identify the peripherals when the hardware has been installed.
  - ➢ **Calibration:** Flight controls are calibrated in-game for precise input.
  - ➢ **View Settings:** The outside and cockpit views will be modified according on your physical configuration, which may include field of view and camera angles.
  - ➢ **Home Cockpit Mode:** This feature in MSFS 2024 allows for more precise control over cockpit interactions and views.
- ✦ **Boost Realism with Accessories:** To enhance your immersion, think about including:
  - ➢ **Add-on Aircraft:** Flying may be more realistic with high-fidelity aircraft models.
  - ➢ **Scenario Enhancements:** Visual realism may be increased with add-ons that improve the environment and airport features.
  - ➢ **Weather and Environment Mods:** These may enhance the immersion by simulating realistic weather patterns and environmental impacts.
- ✦ **Become a Member of the Flight Simulation Community:** Participate in online groups and forums to learn about new advancements, exchange experiences, and solicit advice. Reddit's r/flightsim community and the Microsoft Flight Simulator communities are both helpful communities.
- ✦ **Constant Practice and Learning:** It takes consistent practice and ongoing education to become proficient with a home cockpit setup. To improve your abilities, use online lessons, virtual flying clubs, and even official training courses.

Examining Hardware Compatibility with Third Parties

With improved visuals, more realistic physics, and more aircraft and airports, Microsoft Flight Simulator 2024 introduced much-needed new advancements to the area of flight simulation. The use of third-party technology elevates the simulation's sophisticated features to a far more lifelike experience.

Controls for Flight

The set of flying controls, which includes rudder pedals, throttle quadrants, joysticks, and yokes, is the focal point of every flight simulator configuration. **The majority of them are still supported by MSFS 2024, allowing customers to either upgrade to newer models or keep using their existing gear.**

- **Joysticks and yokes:** MSFS 2024 is typically compatible with them. Manufacturers like Logitech, Thrustmaster, and Honeycomb Aeronautical often provide good examples. For instance, the simulator works well with Honeycomb Bravo Throttle Quadrant and Honeycomb Alpha Flight Controls. To find out whether your particular controller is compatible, it's a good idea to visit the manufacturer's website or forums.
- **Throttle Quadrants:** The Logitech G Throttle Quadrant is one of the throttle quadrants that MSFS 2024 supports. Users report that this configuration is excellent for managing throttle settings while flying.
- **Rudder Pedals:** MSFS 2024 will support rudder pedals made by manufacturers such as Thrustmaster and Logitech. They significantly improve control while taxiing, landing, and departure.

MFDs and Instrument Panels

MFDs and instrument panels may be added to the system for those who like to have a more realistic cockpit. Among the devices that function well with MSFS 2024 are the Saitek Pro Flight Multi Panel and the Logitech G Pro Flight Instrument Panel, which provide real-time control and data display. Realism in such a simulation is further enhanced by tactile input and situational awareness.

Headsets for virtual reality (VR)

Virtual reality provides a level of flight simulation immersion that is hard to match. With the Oculus Rift, HTC Vive, and Windows Mixed Reality headsets, MSFS 2024 does support virtual reality. The user has a 360-degree view of the cockpit and their surroundings. This significantly improves the simulation's realism. Make sure your computer has the specs it needs to run VR software.

Tablets and Flight Management Systems (FMS)

To handle flight plans and systems, advanced users will combine virtual tablets or flight management systems. MSFS 2024 is supported by software like Precision Manuals Development Group's Universal Flight Tablet, which provides a completely integrated interface into flight management. These tools give the simulation more dimensions by providing a wealth of information and control.

Systems for Voice Control

MSFS 2024 already supports speech control technologies, such as SayIntentions.AI, which allow pilots to communicate with the simulator simply by speaking. This adds another element of realism in addition to being quite practical for using features without using your hands.

Considerations for Compatibility

Although MSFS 2024 is compatible with a large number of third-party hardware devices, it is advised to confirm compatibility before making a purchase. Manufacturers and developers often provide updates to make sure their products are compatible with the most recent simulator version. For the most recent compatibility information, official websites and community forums are excellent resources.

Getting on board with Virtual Airlines

Organizations known as virtual airlines use flight simulators to replicate the operations of actual airlines. As a result, they provide pilots the opportunity to attend events, fly on time, and see the more intricate aspects of airline management. The majority of them mimic the layout and operations of an actual airline, including staff coordination, route management, and flight planning.

Advantages of Flying with a Virtual Airline

- **Structured Flight Operations:** By giving pilots the chance to fly a schedule much as they would in the real world, VAs gives the simulation a more realistic feel. Pilots benefit greatly from this in terms of learning and comprehending airline operations and procedures.
- **Community Engagement:** Being a part of a VA fosters a feeling of belonging that introduces you to others who have a similar interest in aviation. This friendship offers the chance for group learning and development.

- **Development of abilities:** When joining a virtual airline, some additional abilities improved include flight planning and communication navigation. Pilot technique may be continuously improved via contact with other pilots and training provided by the majority of virtual airlines.
- **Obtain Unique Items:** The majority of virtual airlines employ specific resources for Custom Liveries Flight Plans and enhance simulators.

Sign Up for a Virtual Airline

The actions:
- **Research and Selection:** Start by researching several virtual airlines in the hopes of identifying one that interests you and fits your degree of expertise. Think about realism, operating zones, and aircraft flow kinds. There are a lot of virtual airlines listed on websites like VA-List, and you may filter them to locate the ones that meet your needs.
- **Application Process:** After determining which VA is best for you, you may check the application process on their official website. This might include completing an application, going through a training program, or showcasing your abilities in a flying simulator.
- **Integration with MSFS 2024:** The majority of VAs have made system updates to enable smooth MSFS 2024 integration. Pilots may conduct VA operations straight from the simulator, and flight data is captured as precisely as feasible. For instance, each trip may add to your virtual airline statistics thanks to FSAirlines' flight tracker, which links your flight simulator with their online crew center.
- **Engagement and Participation:** After enrolling, take an active role in all VA events, training sessions, and planned flights. The secret to optimizing the advantages of joining a virtual airline is engagement.

Well-known Virtual Airlines That Work with MSFS 2024

The well-known virtual airlines listed below provide a variety of experiences and are known to work with MSFS 2024:
- **Fly with Virtual Airlines in the UK:** A reputable virtual airline with a range of aircraft and routes that emphasizes community involvement and authenticity.
- **The Pilot Club:** The Pilot Club provides a variety of aircraft and flying operations and is well-known for its encouraging community and varied training programs.

- **FSAirlines:** offers a framework for managing virtual airlines that is compatible with MSFS 2024 and includes features like crew management and flight monitoring.
- **BOX-Virtual:** A virtual airline based on vAMSYS that offers realistic flying with timetables derived from real life.
- **Virtual Star Alliance:** a virtual airline network that provides a worldwide flying experience and operates under the Star Alliance virtual brand.

Considerations for Selecting a Virtual Airline

- **Realism vs. Casual Flying:** Choose between flying in a very realistic setting and flying more lightly. While some VAs takes pleasure in adhering strictly to real-world protocols, others take a more laid-back stance.
- **Community Size and Activity:** Take into account the VA community's size and degree of activity. There may be more chances for activities and assistance in a bigger, more engaged community.
- **Training and Support:** To improve your abilities, look at VAs that provides in-depth training courses.

Taking Part in Online Competitions and Events

In addition to bringing the community together, the contests and events provide pilots the chance to practice their abilities, compete for rewards, and connect with like-minded individuals from across the globe.

Weekly Fly-Ins with the Community

The "Community Fly-in Friday," which takes place every Friday at 11:00 AM Pacific Time (19:00 UTC), is one of MSFS 2024's fantastic highlights. From novices to experts, all pilots are welcome to participate in this open event and explore new locations, exchange stories, and form friendships. Enjoying the companionship of the flight simulation community, seeing other regions of the globe and having fun are the key goals.

League Mode Challenge

The "Challenge League" feature in MSFS 2024 will let pilots to compete against one another in a variety of tasks, including precise landings, rally races, low-altitude challenges, and many more. In order to give the simulation experience a competitive edge, events will also include some of the most famous races, such the Red Bull Air Races and the Reno Air Races, along with new courses like Roswell.

The 2024 WorldFlight

WorldFlight, a charity event that sees teams fly around the globe for seven days, traveling approximately 40,000 nautical miles and visiting 41 airports, is one of the yearly highlights in the flight simulation community. Teams used full-sized simulators to mimic airplanes such as the Airbus A330 and A320 and the Boeing 777, 747, and 737 when the competition began on November 2, 2024. Among many other organizations, money was also donated for the UK's Lullaby Trust and Australia's Royal Flying Doctor Service. On the participant side, air traffic control was organized using the online network VATSIM, and the flight may be webcast live on Twitch, YouTube, or Facebook.

National Contests for eSTOL

With the launch of National eSTOL events, MSFS 2024 has now hopped on board the rapidly expanding sport of competitive STOL. These online tournaments simulate actual STOL contests, in which pilots may alter their aircraft to perform at their best in short-field situations. Detachable engine cowlings to increase cooling and reduce weight are among the variables that may be altered to represent trade-offs in the actual world. The initiative aims to increase interest in simulation and aviation. It establishes a platform where pilots, both virtual and real, may interact and compete fairly.

Events and Accomplishments each week

Weekly activities that may be repeated for additional credit have been introduced by MSFS 2024 to continually challenge and reward the pilots. With a variety of activities to fit everyone's interests and ability level, these events aim to keep the community active. Accomplishments provide a sense of advancement and acknowledgment, which would encourage pilots to perform well in addition to being more likely to engage often.

Taking Part in Online Competitions and Events

To take part in various tournaments and events, complete these steps:

- **Keep Up to Date:** Keep an eye out for announcements of events and contests on the official website and community forums. Another excellent venue for community-organized events is the Microsoft Flight Simulator Forums.
- **Join and Register:** It's usually simple to sign up for events like the Community Fly-in Friday. Announcements for events often provide information and links to participate.
- **Prepare Your Aircraft:** You will need to set up your aircraft for certain occasions. There are several choices for MSFS 2024, particularly for events like National eSTOL.
- **Join the Community:** To interact with other players, exchange stories, and solicit advice, use social media groups, Microsoft Flight Simulator Forums, and Discord.
- **Practice and Compete:** To do well in contests, consistent practice is necessary. To improve your abilities, take part in practice runs, go over event-specific criteria, and attend training sessions.

The advantages of taking part

Participating in online contests and events has several advantages:

- **Skill Development:** Consistent involvement aids in enhancing navigational abilities, flying proficiency, and knowledge of aircraft systems.
- **Community Building:** Making connections with other enthusiasts promotes a feeling of acceptance and offers chances for cooperation and education.
- **Acknowledgment and Rewards:** For one's efforts and accomplishments, the majority of these events provide a series of accolades, virtual trophies, and sometimes even actual prizes.
- **Realistic Experience:** Participating in organized competitions simulates actual aviation situations, giving participants a far more realistic understanding of real-life difficulties.

Final Thoughts

For both casual gamers and aviation aficionados, Microsoft Flight Simulator 2024 has significantly enhanced the flight simulation genre and added a whole new degree of realism to the product. Aerial firefighting, air search and rescue, and crop dusting are just a few of the additional mission types that provide the player a wide array of difficulties. Additionally, including additional aircraft like as gliders, airships, and hot air balloons will enhance gameplay and accommodate a greater variety of flying styles. Realism has been increased by the MSFS 2024 graphics' greater graphic appeal and more aesthetically pleasing perspectives. Better control over flight dynamics is made possible by its upgraded physics engine, which results in more realistic flights. The simulator's intricacy is increased with live world data, such as real-time flight and marine monitoring, which gives players access to the present world, which is always changing. Players may go through more than 3,000,000 potential mission and task combinations in the game's career mode. This comprises missions and weekly challenges that bring various seasons and weather, resulting in unique flying circumstances for every trip. Wildfires, snow, tornadoes, and auroras are examples of environmental elements that significantly enhance the realism of a virtual flight, which may be very unexpected. Unfortunately, there were significant technical problems with MSFS 2024's launch. Within a few days of its debut, the game received an "Overwhelmingly Negative" rating on Steam due to issues with missing aircraft, excessive loading times, and game crashes. The developers have been attempting to address these issues via updates and server enhancements after admitting that their servers had been overloaded by more gamers than they had expected. Microsoft Flight Simulator 2024 is a huge advancement in flight simulation that appeals to a wide range of users because to its richness and variety. The unique elements and authenticity to actual flying are not obscured by early technological issues, giving this game a promising start that might ultimately lead to new standards in this genre. MSFS 2024 will undoubtedly be the best flight simulator for many years to come thanks to the creators' constant maintenance and improvements.